Soul Construction:

Shape Your Character Using 8 Steps from the Timeless Jewish Practice of Mussar

Ruchi Koval

Library of Congress Control Number: 2021940724

ISBN: 978-1-7370831-0-8

Printed in the United States of America

Dedications

In loving memory of:

Elise Mesh (Esther Faigel bas Silka)

Her life was the embodiment of love for her family, friends, the Jewish people, and the State of Israel.

We will continue to be inspired by her warmth and kindness to all, and by her love of life.

May the lessons and inspiration in this book be an elevation for her beautiful soul.

Sydney and Michael Harris

Akiva Harris

Sarah Rena and Josh Grodko

Chaim Yehuda and Meira Harris

Racheli and Shuey Gordon

Yakov Harris

———

In honor of Ruchi Koval and all other Torah educators dedicated to teaching the beauty of mussar values.

Sheryl and Gerald Hartman

———

In memory of my beloved grandmother, Zina Rosenberg, who embodied true loving-kindness, not just with her own family but with everyone she encountered.

Allison Schultz

In loving memory of:

Reuven ben Aharon, z"l (Robert "Bob" Adams)
Freida Leah "Ginny" Adams-Kafka
Yaakov Kafka
Bayla Ruby Kafka

We sometimes learn more about our parents in their passing than in their life. For my Dad, we learned he was doing so much loving-kindness quietly during his life, helping others to establish a livelihood. His passing accelerated my own journey to Torah observance, and may every mitzvah we do be in his merit.

Ginny Adams

"Appoint a teacher for yourself; acquire a friend for yourself" (Pirkei Avot 1:6)

Dear Ruchi,

I am truly blessed to have you as both my sage teacher and dear friend.

May your work continue to inspire!

With tremendous gratitude,

Sarah bat Tziporah

Table of Contents

New beginnings.
Sharpen those pencils as you peel away old layers, the ones that no longer serve you, the pieces and parts
that have become dried out and brittle.
Underneath is new, living material, to be discovered and used to create something amazing.
This year, we've become vulnerable, our weaknesses exposed.
But that's how you grow strong:
When you let the hard shell fall away.
When you let the soft parts show.
When you're willing to create something that never existed.
When you show your work to someone who might not like it.
Let your strengths propel you forward and let your weaknesses be your guide.
Life is your school.
Be the perpetual student, the one who never grows weary of sharpening her pencils,
of trying again, of showing her work,
of erasing, and always, always starting again fresh. – Ruchi Koval

FOREWORD

How I came to be a rebbetzin

In 1998, at the tender young age of 23, I became a rebbetzin.

What is a rebbetzin? The simple answer is that it is the title given to the wife of a rabbi. But that doesn't tell the whole story. Traditionally, being a rebbetzin is akin to being First Lady. You are no longer an independent, private person. If your husband serves as the rabbi of a community, many responsibilities fall in your lap. This often includes lots of guests at Shabbat (Sabbath) and holiday meals and providing personal counseling and teaching. The community assumes that you are a two-for-the-price-of-one deal or, to put it more delicately, that the two of you are being hired as a team.

Here is my back story: my husband Sruly and I, both raised as Orthodox Jews, married in 1993, when I was 19 and he was 22. We moved to Israel, where he studied ancient Jewish texts at a men's yeshiva (a school for advanced Jewish and Biblical studies) and I worked as a proofreader in an English-language Judaica publishing company. The plan was for us to stay in Israel as long as we could and then come back to our native Cleveland where he would go into business, possibly with his dad.

Three years into this plan, my husband was on a city bus in Jerusalem along with a neighbor of ours. He was an older, German-Jewish gentleman whom we knew only in passing.

"May I share a thought with you?" he asked.

"Sure," my husband politely said.

"My life was saved three times. Twice from the Nazis, and once from terrorists. Life is short, and I say things directly. Just as the Torah teaches that we should give 10% of our earnings to charity, it likewise teaches that we should give 10% of our time to the community."

"Wow," said my husband. "That's a beautiful thought."

"So what are you doing?" the man peered at him.

"Um… well, I'm a full-time religious student and my wife works and we're raising our young kids."

"Do you mean," the man persisted, "that you don't have one hour a week to donate to the community?"

Silence.

Sruly got off the bus, walked into our apartment, and announced to me that he was going to start volunteering at *Aish Hatorah*, an institution of Jewish education for young Jewish adults with limited religious backgrounds. He loved it, the students loved him, and we hosted many of them in our home for Sabbath dinners and holidays. A scant six months after his bus conversation, he strolled through the door and announced that he was going to become a community rabbi.

I greeted this announcement with some reservations. Would I have to be a rebbetzin? I hoped not. Rebbetzins, to my mind, were old and wizened and cooked a lot. I was 21 and cute and hated cooking. He assured me I could remain my usual cute self. Nothing would change.

But everything did.

Sruly enrolled in rabbinical school, and after he graduated and received his rabbinic ordination we moved to Buffalo Grove, Illinois, for his first pulpit position. I was now, officially, a rebbetzin. My own background did include years of elementary and high school Jewish education plus a year of women's religious seminary training that involved full-time Judaic studies, so I did have a certain amount of scholarship, albeit in limited areas. However, I'm not quite sure why anyone listened to a word I had to say back then. I had so little wisdom and personal knowledge about life.

How mussar changed everything

Here I am twenty years later. I'm still cute (I hope) and I still hate cooking. More importantly, I've lived life. I've experienced hardship and diagnoses and setbacks and fear and shame. I've taught hundreds of adults and teens and heard their stories. I've learned about pain and empathy and compassion. I've learned to eat humble pie. I've learned to never say never. I learned how to apply the theoretical knowledge I was privileged to have from Jewish wisdom to real-life practical situations. Several years ago, all of this coalesced when I started to teach *mussar*.

The Mussar Movement began in the 1800s when a Lithuanian rabbi named Israel Salanter revived and organized an ancient path toward spirituality, based on personal ethics and character development. Rabbi Salanter founded this movement in order to focus on refining one's character traits as a primary path toward becoming a Godly person.

Our involvement in teaching mussar happened by accident. My husband and I were teaching a parenting class about how to work on one's marriage, and Sruly mentioned that one of the most important tools in a marriage is mussar—working on one's own character.

After class, Audrey, one of the members of our congregation, approached me and said, "So what's that mussar stuff? Are we doing that? Should we be doing that? Can we do that?"

Now, my husband and I had both studied mussar formally in our religious high schools and during our post high-school education. We had access to the texts, which we'd studied in the original Hebrew. It was part of our upbringing to actively and consciously work on our character traits, such as kindness, patience, generosity, joy, and faith. But until Audrey asked her question, it did not occur to us to teach it to those with limited Judaic or religious background.

I decided to give it a whirl.

Plucking a mussar volume originally written 500 years ago from my bookshelf, I began the work of plowing through the 28 character traits it discussed.

Little did I know how much studying mussar would transform me, the teacher. Little did I know how much I personally would need these mussar lessons in the years to come.

I have learned so much from mussar and from teaching mussar. The women in my classes and who I lead on my trips to Israel are incredible and have enriched my life in many ways. I am honored that they entrust me with their biggest challenges and they have assured me repeatedly that mussar has likewise changed their lives.

Julia is a student of mussar, mother of four, grandmother of two, and has been married almost 34 years. She describes how the study has enhanced her business:

My life has been enriched by studying mussar, because it gave me permission to walk away from negativity. I was working as a personal chef in a toxic home with high levels of ego, gossip, meanness, and negativity. It was making me physically ill. Mussar helped me quit. I'm not a quitter, and this was a very rough decision for me. I fantasized about my exit speech, in which I would point out all the craziness. Thanks to mussar, my exit was much less dramatic. I put my ego to the side and told them, 'I have to leave for personal reasons that at this time I'm not comfortable sharing.'

"But during the four years I had been working with this family, I absolutely was able to help them tame their speech. They called me their angel because, although the environment was still too combative for my nerves, I definitely brought more peace to the home than there had been before. We still communicate with each other, and every time they call me, I'm reminded about another mussar lesson: some people are incapable of change.

She's right, of course. Rabbi Salanter taught: "When I was a young man, I wanted to change the world. But I found it was difficult to change the world, so I tried to change my country. When I found I couldn't change my country, I began to focus on my town. However, I discovered that I couldn't change the town, and so as I grew older, I tried to change my family. Now, as an old man, I realize the only one I can change is myself, but I've come to recognize that if long ago I had started with myself, then I could have made an impact on my family. And my family and I could have made an impact on our town. And that, in turn, could have changed the country and we could all, indeed, have changed the world."

This is one of the most important lessons that my students and I have learned: you can't fix and change other people. Mussar is *only* about fixing and changing yourself. But the secret of mussar is that when you fix and change yourself, it's impossible to not have a quiet, revolutionary impact on those around you. Just ask Julia.

Twenty years after becoming a rebbetzin, I feel I may have finally earned my title. I have learned so much, and Judaism contains so much brilliant wisdom for living that I feel compelled to share it with a broader audience. This book is a taste of the aggregated wisdom I have learned from mussar and from my students. My experience and the feedback I have received over the years tells me that mussar will change your life. It will most certainly change you. And what I have learned, sometimes painfully, is that the only one you can control is you.

How this book will help you

In this book, we will explore eight core character traits that I think are most broadly needed in our relationships with others:

1. Favorable Judgment
2. Forgiveness
3. Accepting Others
4. Generosity
5. Positive Speech
6. Silence
7. Renewal
8. Happiness

Each chapter is based on one of these traits. Like most things in life, they do not fit neatly into boxes but spill over one into another. Nevertheless, focusing on one area at a time is better than trying to make massive changes in many areas. As we focus on improving ourselves with each of these tools, we will also see how, inevitably, changing ourselves will affect our families, friends, and communities.

This is a book that isn't meant to be read so much as it is meant to be studied, practiced, and considered in small doses over time. Changing ourselves so that we internalize and practice mussar is a multi-year process of creating and maintaining new habits and new ways of thinking. Yet, even the very first baby steps can transform our lives. As I hope you will see, mussar is exciting and liberating. It's astonishing, transformative, and therapeutic. I'm excited to share it with you.

And you should listen to me. Because, you know, I'm a rebbetzin.

CHAPTER 1: FAVORABLE JUDGMENT— New Ways of Seeing

I must confess that being judgmental is my default position. The only reason that some people who know me don't think this is true is because I've been working on negating this tendency for years through my study of mussar. But the people who know me best have certainly seen this unflattering side of me. Even if being judgmental is not a primary battle of yours as it is for me, to some degree being judgmental plagues most of us in one form or another. How does one transition from being judgmental to becoming a non-judgmental person?

Judgmentalism is everywhere and crosses all ethnic and religious circles. People are judgmental about whether you're too materialistic or don't care enough about how you or your house looks; too involved in your kids' schoolwork or too chilled about it; too controlling or too laid-back; too fastidious about time or always late; too formal at work or too casual. In politics, the harsh judgmentalism about people with different views has caused terrible social division. Even those of us who are judgmental get annoyed with judgmental people, understandably so. No one likes being judged or criticized.

Who controls your thoughts?

We often assume we don't have control of our thoughts, but that's not true. Some of God's instructions for our lives involve thoughts— "Love your fellow man as yourself,"[1] for instance, or "Don't be jealous."[2] It must stand to reason that we *do* have the ability to regulate our minds. How else could God expect us to do so? He doesn't ask us to do the impossible. Instead, thoughts are like Internet ads. Have you ever clicked on an ad for a lotion and found yourself inundated with similar ads? The same is true for our thoughts. The more attention you give a certain thought, the more of them you get. So we *can* train ourselves to be less judgmental. Knowing why we should do so will make it easier to learn how.

How judging hurts you

Mussar points out that as bad as it feels to be judged, it's even worse for us when we're doing the judging. Since most of us have a much easier time recognizing other people's judgmentalism rather than our own, the first step is awareness.

I am a fixer by nature, and I turn this trait on myself as well as other people. But I have learned that judging and criticizing others, whether by gossiping about them, critiquing them to their faces, or even just thinking about them judgmentally, is a bad idea. It's true that doing so can hurt people, and it's definitely a buzzkill for relationships, but *being judgmental hurts you as a human being more than it hurts anyone else.*

How? First, when you are constantly judging, you are molding yourself into a negative person. Judgmental people condition themselves and strengthen the neural pathways in their brains to see the negativity everywhere they go. What a depressing way to live!

A Jewish legend tells of a man who visited a town to see if he might want to move there. He asked for an appointment with the local rabbi and said, "Tell me, Rabbi, what are the people of this town like?"

The rabbi countered, "What are the people like in the town where you live now?"

The man replied, "Rabbi, they're awful. Why do you think I want to move? They're selfish and only think of themselves! They're rude and cold! It's a horrible place to live."

The rabbi said, "Then I don't think you're going to like living here either, because the people are exactly the same. They're rude, selfish, and cold. I don't think this town is going to be a good fit for you."

"Thank you so much for your advice. I appreciate your honesty," gushed the visitor.

Several weeks passed and another visitor appeared in town, similarly assessing compatibility for an upcoming move. He too visited the rabbi and asked, "Tell me, Rabbi, what is the community like? Tell me about the people so I can decide if I want to move here."

The rabbi said, "Please tell me what the people are like in the place where you currently live?"

The visitor smiled. "They are just wonderful," he said. "What a shame I have to move. They're the kindest, nicest people you could hope to meet. It is such a wonderful community!"

"Well then," beamed the rabbi, "I think you will love our community. As you will see, its residents are just like that."

The man, thrilled to hear this glowing report, left and proceeded to plan his move.

The rabbi's students, who had overheard these conversations, approached the rabbi in confusion. "Why would you tell one visitor that our community is full of terrible people and the next visitor that it's full of wonderful people?"

The rabbi smiled and explained, "The first man only saw negativity in the people of his community. What does that tell me about him? It tells me that he has a sour eye toward the world. He thinks he will leave his community and find another, better one. What he doesn't realize is that he's going to take his 'dirty glasses' wherever he goes. If he moves here, he will see our people with the same slant. People are people. How you look at them determines what you see. The second man sees the positivity wherever he goes, and he'll bring that view to our community too. That is why I told the first visitor that he'll find the same thing here, and I told the second visitor that he will, likewise, see the same thing here. Each will bring himself and his way of looking at the world to his new community.

Research shows that negative experiences affect us even more powerfully than positive ones, so we have to be even more vigilant to keep our minds in a positive place. As Rick Hanson, psychologist and bestselling author puts it, "The brain is like Velcro for negative experiences, but Teflon for positive ones."[3] In the words of psychologist Dr. Richard Boyatzis, "You need the negative focus to survive, but a positive one to thrive."[4]

Negative experiences, research shows, impact us even more powerfully than positive ones.

Looking out for every worst-case scenario is useful for survival when life is harsh, but terrible for satisfying relationships and personal growth. Judging diminishes me as a human being because it conditions my brain to see the bad. This is a very unpleasant way to be in the universe.

Judging also hurts me in another way. When we have a habit of judging others, we carry a heavy burden. In fact, we don't even realize just how heavy that burden is until we give up the judgment and relieve ourselves of it.

An old legend tells about two peasants who approach a river as they walk. There they find a noblewoman arrogantly awaiting two people just like themselves to carry her across the river. They lift her up on her cot and carry her across. With no thanks or acknowledgment, she steps off and departs.

They continue walking for a long while in silence, each one thinking his own thoughts. Finally, the first man sighs in resentment. "How did we let that woman take advantage of us like that?" The second man looks at him and responds, "I put her down a long time ago. Why are you still carrying her?"

How revealing. A grudge is a judgment we choose to carry for a long time.

The Torah, the Five Books of Moses, teaches us not to take revenge and not to bear a grudge.[5] What is the difference? Ancient Jewish wisdom* explains: When your neighbor won't lend you something and therefore you in turn refuse to lend to your neighbor, that is revenge. What is a grudge?

* Rabbi Daniel Lapin coined the phrase 'ancient Jewish wisdom' as a shorthand for the vast body of Torah knowledge.

Imagine that your neighbor turned you down when you asked to borrow her car. A month later she asked to borrow your car since hers was in the shop for repairs. You respond positively to her request but say, "I'm lending you my car even though you didn't lend me yours."[6] Your action is correct, but you are carrying around a begrudging rock in your head and heart. Who are you hurting? Yourself.

We are often blind to the burden we carry when we judge others and maintain grudges. We end up carrying negative associations, negative assumptions, even negative expectations about how we'll be treated in the future. This is all heavy stuff! Imagine if we could put all that down, and if we could say, "It's not mine to judge. I don't know the history or background. It's probably not about me." We would feel liberated! We think we are helping others when we don't judge, but the truth is no one benefits more than us. Absolving ourselves from the burden of judgment is one of the greatest favors we can do for ourselves. Put down the burden. It's heavy, and it's hurting you.

Releasing judgment helps in another, spiritual way. In the Book of Psalms, King David wrote, "God is your guardian, God is your shadow at your right hand."[7] Ancient Jewish wisdom teaches something startling about this verse. God is our mirror in the sense that He mirrors us. Just as your shadow "copies" whatever you do, God mimics how we behave.[8] If we treat others with respect and esteem, God treats us with respect and esteem. If we forgive and forget—give others the benefit of the doubt—God forgives and forgets our misdeeds and gives us the benefit of the doubt, too. Even though He actually knows our deepest thoughts and motivations, He will focus on a positive interpretation of what we do. I absolutely could use positive judgment from God any day of the week! How about you?

We now know three compelling reasons to quit judging:

1. To train ourselves to look at the universe in a happier way.
2. To put down the heavy burden of judgment.
3. To earn greater compassion and leeway from God.

But how do we go about this? How can we think of others more favorably and free ourselves from being harsh and judgmental? Let's work through beginner, intermediate, and advanced levels of leaving our negative judgments behind.

For illustration, I'd like to present the following scenario. I like to walk or jog around my neighborhood with my dog, Wolfie. It's peaceful, I'm doing something healthy, I enjoy the fresh air and the agreeable company of my dog, and I use the time to listen to inspiring audiobooks or podcasts. My neighborhood is pretty and I enjoy the scenery.

There is one house that is jarring to see. The lawn is unkempt and there are toys strewn all over the place. I can't help but be irritated at the unknown homeowner. With no mussar training, this is the noise in my head: *What's the matter with you? You're a blight on the neighborhood! Clean up your stuff, for goodness sakes! How long does it take? I have kids, and I manage to clean up their bikes and toys each evening. I even think: It's not fair that I should have to pass this ugliness each morning! Selfish! Rude! Thoughtless!*

Intellectually and morally, we may know that our neighbor's yard isn't any of our business. But we judge on autopilot.

We do it without even realizing that we are doing it. That's why we need to fight it.

Let's take this same scenario through three levels of judging favorably so you see exactly how this feels in real life.

Beginner Level: *"With righteousness shall you judge your friend."*[9]

At the beginner level, we can counter negative thoughts by constructing a backstory in our heads that would explain and exonerate the behavior. While the story we create is probably fake, it's *possible* that it's true, and this gives us rational permission to judge favorably. In fact, there is likely another, different, backstory that *is* true. We don't know it and may never know it, but it would explain the person's behavior in a more favorable light. Since we don't know that back story (and it is none of our business) we need to construct our own.

In our brains, as soon as we envision a halfway plausible explanation, or even a fantastic hard-to-believe one, we can relax and say, "It doesn't pay to think judgmentally because there is likely a good explanation." By drawing upon our powers of creativity, we relieve and temper our powers of judgment. The more detailed our fictitious story, the more our minds believe that there likely is just such a story. Haven't we all been judged, and wished that others knew the whole story?

Yehudis Samet, a spiritual mentor and teacher of many women in Jerusalem, wrote a book called *The Other Side of the Story* that chronicles true stories of this nature.[10] Each story she relates shows a situation that at first seems to cast a shadow on someone. But when the full story is revealed, sometimes including absolutely incredible circumstances, we see how the favorable interpretation was justified, far more than an initial viewing of the incident would have supposed.

Back to our messy lawn. Since I don't know the homeowners, I can concoct any story I want in my head to excuse them for the yucky lawn and bad neighborliness.

Maybe the homeowner is ill and her kids, unfortunately, have to play by themselves every day after school. Mom and dad are too busy/weak/tired to worry about the lawn. It's the least of their worries! If, God forbid, I was sick, you can bet my lawn would be the last thing on my mind. And I wouldn't want others judging me for it, because I'd be doing the best I could. In fact, instead of judging these homeowners, I should be filled with compassion!

Here's another possibility: maybe the child who lives here has special needs and the parents try so hard to get the kid to clean up but it's tough. They don't want to just do it themselves because that would be bad parenting. Even though it doesn't look good to the neighbors, their first allegiance is to their child's well-being, neighbors be damned! Anyone with an understanding about special needs, myself included, knows that sometimes you just have to do right by your kid, despite knowing that you will be criticized.

Yet another scenario: maybe it's the husband's job to clean up every night and the wife works full-time and they can't afford help, and she's overwhelmed, and she yells at him and he's also overwhelmed and they fall into bed exhausted each night and the lawn is the last item on their "hon-ey-do" list. Their marriage is suffering, they have no money, and no one cares about the lawn. By the time my imaginary story is developed, I want to pay for a gardener!

Each of these thought experiments leaves the judgmental person far more compassionate toward his subject than before. And, as I discussed at the beginning of this chapter, compassion is a far better choice *for you.* Conducting these thought experiments will help mold you into a more positive thinker and therefore a happier person, relieve you from the burden of anger and criticism, and earn you spiritual favor from God.

What happens when you do know the homeowner? You know that no one is sick and no one has special needs and their jobs are doing fine? You know too much and it's not looking good. Now is the time to get creative in your favorable judging.

If you know the people involved, some of your poetic license is unavailable, so you'll just have to dig deeper. (I did not promise this would be easy, just that it would be worth it.) But how well do we really know them? Everyone we know has stuff going on behind closed doors. It is really hard, and therefore the best proving ground for growth, to dig beneath the surface, *especially when you think you know the score.* Our goal is self-development, so the job of judging others favorably—precisely when it's difficult—is the greatest kind of project.

What could we conjure up now? Not sick, not overwhelmed, all good?

Maybe someone *is* sick and no one knows. Maybe it's embarrassing or they don't want to worry the kids or lose their jobs so they're keeping it quiet. Maybe there's some kind of mental illness and, unfortunately, the stigma is preventing them from letting people know. Maybe there's abuse going on. The bottom line is that we actually have no idea what is going on in another person's life. Even when we know, we don't know. There are many reasons that people keep their issues private, and if we knew what others were struggling with, we'd give them a huge hug instead of a boatload of judgment. As the sage Hillel taught, "Don't judge your friend until you have stood in his place."[11] You can never really stand exactly where another person stands.

If we knew what others were struggling with, we'd give them a huge hug instead of a boatload of judgment.

But the most simple (and often true) explanation is this: you're right, they're wrong. They made a mistake. They are not perfect. They forgot, they didn't realize, they goofed. And do you know what? So do you, and so do I, albeit in different areas. I may be a lawn champion but always bring 15 items to the 12-items-or-less line at the grocery store. I may be a checkout line stickler but talk too loudly on my cell phone while in public. Maybe I have great phone manners but am a terrible email replier. We've all got our foibles! Because we are all imperfect humans!

In Yiddish there's a great word for an idiosyncrasy: *mishugas.* It literally means craziness. I'll be nice about your kind of crazy and you'll be nice about my kind of crazy. I'll be nice about your *mishugas* and you'll be nice about my *mishugas.*

Sound good? Good. After a while, this beginner level will start to feel natural. Let's see if we can dig even deeper and move to an intermediate level.

Intermediate Level: *"A person is obligated to bless God for the bad just as he blesses Him for the good [because it's all good]."*[12]

To present the intermediate level, I have the honor of introducing you to my great-grandfather (seven generations back), the Chassidic master Rabbi Levi Yitzchok of the town of Berditchev, known by his followers as "the Berditchover." He became known by the moniker "defender of Israel" because he would compose passionate prayers defending the Jewish people to God and even 'strike deals' with God to protect and help them. In short, he was a professional spiritual criminal defense attorney.

The Berditchover's brand of good judgment was like none other. He would pinpoint *exactly what looked bad* about a person and turn it around, showing that what looked bad was actually good. Precisely where others saw darkness, he saw light. Where others saw death, he saw life. As opposed to the beginner level where a concocted backstory makes the wrongdoing look good, here we will see that the "wrongdoing" itself is beautiful.

Here is a classic story told of my ancestor, the Berditchover Rabbi: He was once traveling with his entourage of students in a horse and wagon. They passed by a religious Jew wrapped in his holy prayer clothes (his prayer shawl and phylacteries), lying in the mud, fixing his wagon wheel. The students were upset about the disrespect for the holy garments and expressed their feelings to their rabbi. In classic form, the Berditchover turned his face heavenward and said, "Master of the Universe! Look at Your people! They are so attached to you that even when they are fixing their wagon wheel, they simply can't bear to take off your holy garments!"

The Berditchover Rabbi looked at the exact same "bad" thing that his students saw and found good instead! The very thing that made the encounter so irritating to his students was in the holy rabbi's eyes an exonerating influence.

How would this approach look with my lawn issues?

Through my judgmental lens, the toys and overgrown lawn are a sign of blight, neglect, and rudeness. At a beginner level I tried to find a good excuse for the bad behavior. Here at the intermediate level, I can choose to look at the toys and see something else entirely—something that would make the excuse unnecessary altogether. What could I see?

Maybe I could look at the lawn and see parents playing with their kids. Maybe I imagine the healthy, active children playing happily instead of being hindered by parents who are busy worrying about the landscaping. Maybe I could see life, love, and happiness in those toys. Toys, mess, and wrappers are a sign that joy happened here. I'm no longer irritated by the messy lawn. Seeing it makes me smile and feel glad as I picture the happy family it represents.

Are you ready to see how an advanced level of judgment might look?

Advanced Level*: "Beloved is man, for he was created in the image of God."*[13]

In the advanced level of judging favorably, we are going to do something radical. *We are going to look through the bad as though it is invisible.* Therefore we will neither excuse it (beginner) nor see it differently (intermediate). Instead, we are going to see right through it.

To do this, imagine a wall of windows overlooking a beautiful garden. If the windows are clean, you won't even notice them, because you'll be looking right through them to the beautiful greenery beyond. If the windows are dirty, you will focus on the spots on the windows, and the greenery will fade into the background.

This secret to seeing this way is called unconditional love. We all do this selectively. Think of someone you love. Now ask yourself, does this person have faults? The answer is yes, because every human being is flawed. *But loving someone means paying more attention to their virtues than to their flaws.* Notice that this is a choice. You may love your best friend and also acknowledge that she is flighty, forgetful, and perpetually late. Nonetheless, you chuckle at her weaknesses (and adjust your behavior to compensate for hers) because mainly, she's a cool person in your eyes. The beautiful attributes are front and center; the flaws in the background. Put another way, you are looking straight through the "window" of the faults to see the beauty that lies beyond.

Loving someone means paying more attention to their virtues than to their flaws.

Some people look at rebellious teens and see rudeness, disrespect, and irresponsibility. Others have the gift of seeing through all that muck to the shining self beneath. Some people look at their bosses and see rude egotistical aggression. Others see assertiveness and leadership.

Jewish mysticism teaches that every person has a shining self, deep inside. Every human being has a beautiful soul, a shining spark of God.[14] Yet life can layer on something known in kabbalistic sources as "*klippah,*" a hard shell of "otherness" that conceals and darkens the beauty.[15] People who are advanced-level favorable judges have cultivated a talent to see through that hard shell. It's like having spiritual X-ray vision. All they can focus on is the bright light of the soul shining beyond the smudges and spots.

When we look at rude people and see sad, hurt human beings who are just trying their best, we know we have made it to the advanced level. When we see irresponsibility or laziness and look through it and discover kindness, creativity, and joy, we are accessing advanced-level purity. When we see a messy lawn and look just beyond it to the beautiful flowers, we are doing advanced work.

Obstacles to judging favorably

The reason it is so hard to manage that judgmental voice in your head is that there are real obstacles to cultivating this character trait. What are they?

A lot of people leap to judgment because they are insecure. When we're on a sure footing in our relationships, when we are confident and feel loved, we assume the best about others. But when we're feeling shaky, we see threats everywhere. We misinterpret every text message or terse comment, taking offense at what we perceive is an insult of some sort. No wonder we're so ready to jump to anger and assume the worst about others.

Arrogance can also get in the way of judging favorably. It takes a serving of humble pie to acknowledge that you only see part of the picture, that you don't know everything, and that you may have misunderstood. If you've ever self-righteously jumped to conclusions only to be brought to your knees later with new information or new awareness, you know how much you wish you would have given the benefit of the doubt.

I remember once visiting family in New Jersey and trying to get a hold of a friend to let her know I was in town. I called, texted, left voicemails, and received no response. I found myself getting triggered with all kinds of emotions: *Doesn't our relationship matter to her? Why am I the one who always has to follow up with everyone?* (Notice the insecurity here.) Then came the arrogance: *Well, I ALWAYS answer my texts and voicemails. I always return my calls. Guess some people are just flakier than me.*

Thanks to my mussar training, I did not leave a passive-aggressive voicemail but instead remembered to give the benefit of the doubt. *Maybe something happened to her phone. Maybe there's some kind of emergency. Maybe she's not glued to her phone like I am. Maybe she's lovable despite this.* I thought of a beautifully old-fashioned solution and called her on her home phone. And she answered. And told me that her phone had fallen into a lake and was gone, gone, gone.

Boy, was I grateful that I surmounted the obstacles of insecurity, anger, and arrogance and gave her the benefit of the doubt. By the way, we had a perfectly lovely visit.

Remember, you benefit the most when you can find better ways to handle your internal judgy voice. Seeing the good in others instead of the bad is such a lovely liberty. It also takes time, practice, and grit. But it can be done. And it is worth it.

Hallie, a successful wardrobe consultant and Instagram influencer, and a wife and mother of three, has been learning mussar with me for nearly fifteen years. Here's her take:

When I think about how studying mussar changed me, it takes a lot of brainpower. Why? Because the transformation, while pronounced and significant, has been completely subtle at the same time.

I kind of wish I could take a before-and-after picture like people do when they go on diets or new exercise regimens. I wish that was possible with mussar.

In the many years since I began studying with Ruchi, the impact of this type of supportive, non-judgmental, action-based self-evaluation has had a positive ripple effect on so many aspects of my life. My family, my relationships, and my business have all blossomed while navigating life through a mussar lens.

About 18 months after mussar came into my life, I had this conversation with my mom:

She asked, "Have you started taking Prozac?"

"No, why?"

"You just seem happier"

"I am, it's mussar!"

Trust me, I was not miserable before, but viewing things through the lens of mussar has made the sweet sweeter, and the yucky more palatable. When learning the lessons, they seem completely practical and even obvious, and yet it requires learning and re-learning them in order for them to become second nature—and BIG disclaimer —sometimes they're more second nature than others. And some lessons are easier to integrate than others.

Mussar has helped me to embrace that I'm a work in progress and that is okay! And by embracing that in myself, it's allowed me to embrace it in others as well. It has allowed me to stop viewing everything in black and white and to see things on a continuum instead, and that brings me peace.

My job as a personal stylist and wardrobe consultant means that people, both clients and community members, even family for that matter, think I'm judging what they're wearing. BUT, I SOOOO AM NOT! When I started my business, I knew that having a critical eye was an important trait, but mussar has helped me use it for the good.

When I was in elementary and high school, I would get so angry with myself because without meaning to, I'd focus on the one thing that was visually out of place. The girls' socks that were uneven, one braid being thicker than another, colors not matching. It was both a gift and a curse.

What a crappy feeling to go through life; always judging and criticizing other people, especially on how they look.

Thankfully, I can now literally turn my critical eye on and off. And it no longer drives me bonkers! My critical eye is a tool and I use it for a specific purpose. When I'm working with a client, I'm able to focus and turn that eye on, but in a non-judgmental, helping, "bring out your best self" kind of way. Again, I think mussar has helped in the way I deliver the message as well. And then when the session is over, I put the tool away, until it's needed again.

Can you imagine if a plumber walked around all day every day with his plunger at the ready, just in case? When I am out and about in my daily life, I am not thinking about what other people are wearing, especially if I know them. I'm thinking either how happy I am to see them, or of the long to-do list I have to accomplish.

There is one caveat though… When I am out of town, like in Las Vegas or NYC, I turn it on to learn. I love to see what people are wearing and why it works or doesn't work on their body. But that usually happens while sitting in a hotel lobby or on the subway. I also turn it on when awards season is happening. It's a tool for my job, to use when needed.

Mussar has helped me learn how to better use that tool and how I can be in charge of it, not allowing it to be in charge of me.

CHAPTER 2: FORGIVENESS—A Gift to Others as Well as Ourselves

Forgiveness is a state of mind. Along with learning to judge favorably, forgiveness ultimately affords mental freedom. Like judgment, we think of forgiveness as a gift we grant to others, but more than that, it is a gift to ourselves.

Forgiveness is an art, not a science. You'll see families torn apart because forgiveness cannot be found for some affront which can no longer be remembered. Then you'll hear of a Holocaust victim forgiving the Nazis, or a victim of abuse forgiving her abuser. It's hard to make sense of the process, but let's try.

In the first chapter we discussed how carrying grudges and making judgments cause us to carry around pain. If we're not careful, the build-up of grudges and judgments can make us feel like victims, and we may even define ourselves that way. We saw how this harms us. What happens, though, when the offense isn't something as trite as someone not lending us her car, but something that cuts much deeper? The ability to forgive is complex, because the grudge, fueled by pain, is often the only weapon available to a victim. No one can mandate forgiveness. It has to happen in its own sweet time.

There will always be people in our lives who will say and do things that will hurt us deeply. We will be guilty of the same thing, even when we are unaware of the harm we are doing. We are perfect souls with complex brains, housed

We are perfect souls with complex brains, housed in imperfect bodies. in imperfect bodies. Because we are imperfect, we need to learn the art of forgiveness.

Torah origins of forgiveness

The classic Jewish story of forgiveness begins with the tragic story of the sin of the Golden Calf, and spans three months until it reaches its climax on the holiest day of the Jewish year, Yom Kippur. More than 3,300 years ago, Moses descended Mount Sinai with the long-awaited tablets on which the Ten Commandments were written.[1] To his horror, at the bottom of the mountain he saw the Jewish people dancing around the representation of their slipped faith, the Golden Calf. In utter fury and despair, Moses shattered the holy tablets. The Jewish people were in big trouble.

God was fed up with His people. They had wavered in their faith. They had complained. They had earned the dubious moniker of a "stiff-necked people." (Over the years, we've managed to turn it into a compliment—we call it chutz-pah). But this level of rebellion against God was unprece-dented. What had happened? Simply put, the Israelites had counted the forty days until Moses was expected to return, but their count was incorrect. For that reason, they lost hope of Moses' return.

"Moses," said God, "I'm done with them. I'm going to wipe them out and start over with you." To which Mo-ses replied, "God, if you do not forgive them, erase me from the Book that you have written!" For weeks, Moses begged God to forgive his flock—the same flock that had given both God and Moses so much aggravation. In the end, on the day that would become Yom Kippur, three months after the debacle, God forgave the Jewish people, Five days later, He drew them close with the holiday of Sukkot, when He shielded them in a protective embrace.[2]

This story impacts me very powerfully. Forgiveness is stitched into the very fabric of the universe.

Do you forgive me? How we can learn to apologize

Many people don't understand the purpose of an apology, and that makes us not very good at apologizing. People tend to think of apologies as something you need to do to make sure your side of the street is clean. I apologized, I did mine, now I can wash my hands of the affair. Check the box and move on.

But what are apologies for? Jewish texts teach us something surprising and novel. *The goal of an apology is to obtain forgiveness.* Maimonides, a medieval scholar of Jewish wisdom, says that an apology must be designed to be *mefayes*—to appease.[3] In other words, the point of an apology should be to soften the heart of the one who is angry with you, so that they will want to forgive you. It's your job not just to follow a script, but to effectively convince the other person that you are sincere, that you've changed, that you now understand something you didn't previously understand. The person receiving your apology must see that you are contrite and remorseful and that the chances of anything like this happening again are very low.

In this way, you can ask the most important question of your apology: *do you forgive me?* Hopefully, when done correctly, the answer will be yes. That's the point of an apology.

Effective apologies must be designed to maximize the chances of forgiveness, but so many miss the mark. For example, here is my least favorite type of apology: "I'm sorry if…" Any apology that has the word "if" in it is not an apology. It doesn't even contain a basic admission of guilt! "If" means, maybe I did something wrong, maybe I didn't. Maybe *you* think I did, but mostly that's because you're wrong and oversensitive. The word "if" does not belong anywhere in an apology.

Any apology that has the word "if" in it is not an apology.

Here is another way to ruin an apology: "I'm sorry that… but…" This style includes an admission of guilt but it's immediately invalidated by the qualifier "but." "But" means I am offering an excuse that lets me off the hook. I had a good reason and therefore you shouldn't be mad. If you shouldn't be mad, I don't need your forgiveness. "But" can also mean, "I did something wrong but so did you, and therefore you have no claim." That is not helpful! When the issue on the table is your role in the drama, stay focused on that. You can discuss the other person's portion of guilt in a separate conversation.

I sometimes find it useful to explain what could have led me, an obviously flawless human being, to do something so stupid that it demands an apology. But there's a big difference between a reason and an excuse. A reason is this: *I thought it made sense at the time, so I wasn't trying to be terrible. I see now how misguided I was, and it won't happen again.*

An excuse is an attempt to escape culpability by pointing to the reason you did it, or worse, to twist the victim into the role of the aggressor for overreacting: *It made sense to me at the time, so you shouldn't be so mad.* That may be a subtle difference, but it is a significant one.

According to Jewish guidelines, a proper apology is this: "I am sorry that..." followed by filling in what you did wrong. Judaism offers a user-friendly formula for repentance, and one of the most important ingredients is verbal admission of guilt.[4] If you cannot articulate verbally what you did wrong, you do not deserve anyone's forgiveness. There will also be little chance of rehabilitation because you're not even clear about where you went wrong. How can you regret something you don't even realize you did? When you apologize, be careful not to dilute your remorse with excuses nor to compromise it with counterattacks.

Finally, conclude with the most important part. You must ask the other person, "Do you forgive me?"

Since earning forgiveness is the ultimate goal of offering an apology, set the stage for success. Talk in a private setting, unless another key person might enhance the experience. Try to make the timing optimal. Before you start, you might ask yourself, "What is the likelihood that my apology will achieve the goal of earning forgiveness?" Perhaps you should bring a peace offering of a gift, flowers, or a card. Maybe the apology should be written, instead of in a conversation. Different approaches have different pros and cons, and you have to consider how you will best present your case. You also have to consider how receptive you think the other person will be to your choice of presentation. Again, the goal is forgiveness, so do what you can to bring that goal into reality.

What if we are not forgiven? Judaism teaches that if we are denied forgiveness at first, we must try two more times to appease and soften the other person and convince them that we really have reformed. Often, the day of apology is not the day of forgiveness. Forgiveness is a big deal. People need time to process their emotions. We may feel nervous while we are waiting for our second (or third) chance at bat, but we want those we have hurt to genuinely forgive us, not just utter an insincere or grudging forgiveness to end the conversation.

What happens when the person we wronged is no longer capable of forgiving us? I have a friend who had a terrible relationship with her mother-in-law, a Holocaust survivor. The older woman was scarred and traumatized. Her way of coping was to live a narcissistic life. After many years, my friend realized that her own reactivity also played a role in their poor interactions. She sometimes went for months without talking to her mother-in-law, and over time, she felt deeply sorry. One year before Yom Kippur, the Jewish Day of Atonement, she was feeling particularly guilty about her share in their damaged relationship. Her mother-in-law had already died. What could my friend do?

She decided to follow the directions of Maimonides (the medieval rabbi and scholar I referenced earlier) and assembled a quorum of ten at the graveside, in Israel, to hold a "formal" ceremony asking the deceased for forgiveness. She prayed and confessed to her mother-in-law, "I'm sorry that I didn't honor you the way you deserved. You are now in the World of Truth, and you know how relationships work. I am so sorry for my share of the problem."

The quorum recited, in Hebrew, *"You are forgiven, you are forgiven, you are forgiven!"* Their solemn declaration echoed off the cold Israeli gravestones, as if to respond. Although she could not formally obtain verbal forgiveness from someone who had passed, the experience was just as cleansing. She felt a palpable sense of freedom from anger. The effects have seeped into so many other relationships in her life, allowing her to notice relationships in which she would have previously been similarly triggered, and instead to choose to engage in the relationship with serenity and forgiveness.

Since it is uncomfortable to think about the people whom we may have wronged and to whom we owe apologies, Yom Kippur is an important annual opportunity for Jews to cleanse ourselves of these hidden burdens, and to offer and receive forgiveness. The ideas surrounding this holiday are useful for everyone. They teach us that it's our responsibility to ponder if there's anyone who harbors resentment toward us. If so, we need to find them and ask for forgiveness. This takes moral courage. Of late, I've noticed that many people have taken to social media with generic posts before Yom Kippur such as, "I hope you all forgive me if I've done anything to upset you!" (There's that poisonous "if.") I'd grade that apology a C-. Which Facebook "friends" will decide to offer forgiveness from a post like that? I'd guess few, if any.

Other posts I've seen are much more effective. Here's an example: *"I interact with many people in my job, and I know sometimes I hurt others' feelings. If you are one of those people, please send me a private message so we can talk about it and I can make it right."*

While it is our job to seek out those we have harmed and appease them, often we don't even know who harbors resentment against us. For this reason, I give the above type of Facebook post, inspired by my friend Adrienne Gold, an A. It leverages modern technology to connect human beings. It invites uncomfortable conversations and opens up both parties to feeling vulnerable. It also ups the chances of forgiveness.

On my last women's mission to Israel with Momentum, a trip especially designed for Jewish moms, I stood up on the last day and told the women, "I have been teaching and guiding you for eight days. I'm sure I've said things that have hurt or offended you or that have touched on sensitive areas. Please allow me the opportunity to make it right by coming up to me to discuss it."

I learned the need for such a statement several years earlier when I was the guest speaker at a spiritual weekend retreat in Los Angeles. The retreat was for women who had previously been on a Momentum trip, and I was giving a talk about parenting. I commented that some kids are "orchid kids," meaning they need a lot of maintenance and care, and sometimes even in the most favorable circumstances they fail to thrive. On the other hand, some kids are like dandelions, which seem to bloom no matter where they're planted. I made a joke about orchids, and about how I never seem to be able to keep them alive. I said, "I can keep kids alive, but I can't seem to keep plants alive."

Three women came over to me after the lecture. They thanked me for the lecture, but told me that there was a message they felt I needed to hear as I am a public speaker and therefore have an important platform. They were all bereaved mothers, and alerted me to the fact that joking about keeping kids alive was not sensitive, as bereaved parents often blame themselves and feel wracked with guilt for being unable to save their children. This was obviously a very sobering thing for me to hear, and I thanked them for it. You can be sure I never made that joke again, and I've learned how easy it is to be hurtful on a public platform without meaning to.

Up until now, we've been looking at apologies from the standpoint of the offender. Now let's now turn things around and examine the issue from the perspective of someone who has been wronged.

Obstacles to forgiveness

Just as there are people who we may have harmed but we are totally unaware of it, there are also those who have harmed us and they may be equally oblivious to it. How is forgiveness possible when a person has no idea of the hurt they have caused? Can we forgive, and should we forgive, those who have never apologized?

Even in the absence of an apology, it is in our best interests to forgive. Although we are used to thinking that forgiveness is a gift to another person—and it is—there's a lot more to it than that. The other person needs your forgiveness to move on and to stand before God to atone for the misbehavior which has sullied his or her spiritual slate. But you need it as well. Forgiving others is a gift to yourself. Harboring resentment, pain, and grudges, especially when waiting for another person to apologize, is like being stuck at a rest stop on a journey. You're on your way to somewhere else, but you cannot move forward because you think it's the other person's problem. Truthfully, your problem is in your hands.

Dr. John E. Sarno, in his bestselling book *Healing Back Pain,* contends that back pain is often a manifestation of emotional distress that can go unrecognized by the sufferer.[5] When people are not emotionally available to deal with their pain, it becomes physical pain. Emotional pain, he contends, often manifests as back or neck pain, knee pain, headaches, stomach issues, and rashes. I sometimes get eczema and even hives when I'm in emotional distress. When the lockdown began in the Coronavirus pandemic of 2020, I developed severe sciatica.

People who are unaware of this dynamic, though, never seek help. They think they are okay. They swallow everything inside, and don't legitimize their pain. Their brains are so overtaxed with this squashed pain that it becomes physical pain, though the source is emotional. People who harbor resentments can deal with this pain via forgiveness. Forgiveness is a gift to yourself because you don't want your brain and your body to be filled with poison.

Thousands of years before Dr. Sarno developed his theory, King Solomon described the toll that unresolved emotions can have on the body: "The rotting of the bones is envy."[6] Left unchecked, difficult emotions, such as envy and grudges, can literally eat you up on the inside.

Aside from our obliviousness to the need to seek forgiveness, and the human tendency to want to hold grudges, there is another obstacle to issuing forgiveness. Sometimes we think, somewhat arrogantly, that we should be above normal human emotions. It's hard to admit that our feelings have been hurt and that others have the power to weaken us. We may even feel this is a shameful flaw. Perhaps we think it's juvenile to admit these feelings. If we're angry at someone or hurt or jealous, it burns within us and is released externally as anger and gossip. We might follow the comfortable route of behaving in a passive-aggressive manner, or even plain old aggressive.

Bottom line, if you want to heal you have to get to the source of the "inflammation." Name the emotion and recognize it so you can let it go. There's nothing shameful about that. You have to feel it to heal it.

When a little kid going to sleep thinks the shadow is the bogeyman, Mom turns on lights to show him that it's just a chair or a teddy bear. Suddenly everything is less scary. Meeting your intimidating boss for the first time seems totally daunting. Then you get to know him or her a little as a real human being. The light of humanity starts to dawn. The same is true of our emotional realities. We need to turn up the lights and see what's really going on so we can be at peace.

We have to call pain what it is. We have to identify people who have hurt or harmed us. We must admit that certain people cause us emotional pain. We're used to saying, "I'm fine," but it's rarely true. I often joke, "If a woman says she's fine, call 911." I've learned that the word "fine" is the biggest indicator that someone isn't talking about his or her feelings. Someone's not turning up the lights on the pain.

Once we've taken these preliminary steps of feeling, acknowledging, and naming our pain, we are ready to move through the steps of forgiveness.

The six steps of forgiveness

Step 1: Identify one person who has caused you anger or pain and write the name and event down. You have not forgiven them yet. Chances are pretty good they haven't approached you three times to obtain your forgiveness. For right now, that's not the point. The point is noticing what that pain is doing to you. What can you do to move past it, for your own sake?

Step 2: Ask yourself, "Am I interested in moving past this pain? Am I willing to get comfortable with the idea and really consider it?" It can be a long process, and no one can tell you how long or how short this process will be. So much depends on what has been perpetrated. Is it still happening?

Is it happening consistently? Is this person still in your life? Does this person still have the power to hurt you?

When you have finished Step 2, you should be comfortable with the concept of arriving at the place of forgiveness. Sometimes we may get stuck before we reach Step 2, unwilling or unable to get comfortable with the idea of forgiveness. That's all right. We will take our time and periodically check in with ourselves to see if we've moved slightly ahead, if we are ready to move toward the idea of forgiveness.

Saying "I forgive you" is as powerful as saying "I love you." These are profoundly significant words and should not be uttered lightly. It is giving the gift of soul to another human being who has harmed you. It's a precious commodity and one should not forgive before the action will be authentic. If you are asked for forgiveness outright but you are not ready, you can say, "I appreciate your apology but I am not ready to forgive just yet. I need more time."

Saying "I forgive you" is as powerful as saying "I love you."

Step 3: Arrive at the awareness that forgiving the other person is the right thing to do, even if you'd still rather not. It might sound like this: "Yeah, it's the right thing to do. Nope, I'm not ready to do it." That's a step. In theory forgiving is a good thing to do, but you're not there yet. You're conscious of the fact that you don't want to live in that place of pain and resentment anymore. You want to be free. At this point, it's not an "if" you are going to forgive, but rather a question of how and when, and what that conversation will look like.

You may find yourself thinking at this stage, *I don't need to forgive. They don't deserve it.* Perhaps this is true, but what if you do it anyway? Or, what if you admit that it's the right move for you, but you're simply not ready? What if you forgive because YOU deserve to be free of this prison and not because others deserve it? Sometimes when you don't feel like doing something you convince yourself that it doesn't need to be done. Try to overcome this bias and push yourself forward in the act of forgiveness. It will bring healing powers to your emotions and even your body.

Step 4: Cultivate the ability to look past the hurt. The vast majority of relationships have some redemptive blessing. Often, people are simply doing the best they can with the tools they have. There may still be so much to gain from the relationship. Can you look past the hurt and see the blessing?

Remember our tools about judgmentalism from Chapter 1? Maybe the person who hurt you had a bad upbringing. Maybe he grew up with overly controlling parents or with trauma, and is not emotionally healthy. Remember that giving others the benefit of the doubt is even more a gift to oneself than to the other person. Ask yourself if this person has brought any degree of goodness to your life, performed favors, taught you anything, or been there for you? Can you harness any of that?

This process takes a lot of inner strength and honesty. In the physical realm, people set high goals for themselves such as running marathons or hiking mountains. I sometimes wonder about how and why people set these extreme goals (my most ambitious physical goals usually include walking 10,000 steps a day). They set a goal, divide it into small chunks, get the right training, and thereby achieve exceptional levels of fitness. Perhaps we can consider similar goals for ourselves spiritually and emotionally. It's certainly worth our time and effort. Train for as long as you need. Get coaching and support. Congratulate yourself on every step.

Overall, do this for yourself. Sometimes the other person will not even know or care.

Step 5: Once you've acknowledged that the person or relationship has redemptive value, your feelings of hurt have now begun to give way to forgiveness. Feelings of pain have dissipated somewhat so you can manage them. Believe that others are doing the best they can. In truth, we never really know, so we may as well guess compassionately. Only God knows what people are contending with, and which temptations are too great for them. Other people are not us.

It also doesn't matter if the slight was big or small. What matters is what kind of emotional pain it causes you. Certainly, you shouldn't let your boundaries down and let the other person hurt you again and again. We can forgive and still be smart about our future relationships. Some relationships are healthiest at a distance.

Forgiving is not the same as forgetting. When you've reached forgiveness, you can see the other person and remember what happened, but you won't feel the pain and anger anymore. You won't *Forgiving is not the same as forgetting.* define yourself as a victim. You won't feel the need for revenge or gossip, and you can even converse like a normal person.

Step 6: The feelings of resentment have now given way to true forgiveness.

The book *Ethics of the Fathers* has some insights for us on the subject. This classic work is a compendium of Jewish wisdom (composed c.190 - c.230 CE) that contains ethical guidance handed down from Moses to Joshua. Its advice was passed on to each subsequent generation of Jewish leaders. Although it's a relatively short, six-chapter volume, it is incredibly rich with moral truisms and spiritual food for thought. In one example, Rabbi Mathia ben Charash teaches that we should try to be the first to initiate peace.[7] When two people have a standoff, each should say, "I should be the first to make peace." What if we would each reach out to someone with whom we've quarreled, and asked to start over? What if we were the first to apologize and bring down the barriers?

I am a generally calm person, but there was one time in my life that I remember actively yelling at another adult. This person was in a position of authority at my kid's school and didn't handle my child well. I kept it in all year (in hindsight, probably a dumb plan). On the last day of the school year, issues came to a head and, over the phone while standing at a gas station pumping gas into my minivan, I yelled at this person passionately in a way that was equal parts mortifying and delicious: "I really don't think you care that much about kids! If you cared about kids this never would happen! No! You care about your school and its image!

How could you leave a kid with this memory on his very last day in your care!?"

Time passed and the memory of my rage faded. But then, one night I was teaching a mussar class to my group in Cleveland and we arrived at this teaching of *Ethics of the Fathers*. I assigned the task of finding someone with whom you've clashed and going to apologize.

I realized I'd have to do the homework myself. I'd have to walk the walk and be the first to apologize. Memories of my tantrum returned to me in full color. Reluctantly, although I still thought this person deserved my upset, I sent an email, following the guidelines I've shared with you for obtaining forgiveness. I said I wanted to apologize for my bad behavior, and that I didn't usually scream at people. I had felt very hurt and therefore behaved wrongly. I said I hoped he/she would forgive me.

I got a nice response. The person understood and also expressed being sorry for things he/she had done. I didn't say, "I forgive you," because the person didn't ask for forgiveness. To be honest, neither did I. I was still too angry to humble myself that much, and only said that I hoped there would be forgiveness. It took me nine more months to forgive that person in my heart. Now when I see this person I am struck by the awareness of how poorly suited this person is for the field of education, but I am no longer consumed with anger.

See how long the process takes? It was more than just an assignment. It was more than just an email. This was a real emotional journey that could not be rushed, but eventually,

I achieved resolution. I fully believe that people like this educator believe they're acting in my kids' best interests. They are often doing the best they can with the (limited and dull) tools they have. But in my moment of pain, I couldn't even acknowledge that. All I saw was a fire in front of my eyes.

Also forgive yourself

Since we are talking about our own inner world, I must mention here that everything we have learned about forgiveness applies equally to forgiving oneself. We all make mistakes and we all have regrets. Often, we are our own worst critics. We say horrible, self-recriminating things to ourselves that we would never say to others: "You're such a loser! You always mess up. You're a terrible friend." When we love ourselves enough to forgive ourselves, we often feel worthy of extending that love and forgiveness to others.

It can take time to work these thoughts and emotions out of your system. Just as physical processes take time, just as physical wounds need a healing process, our hearts and souls are no different. Respect the process. The mind is powerful, and learning to manage our thoughts and emotions is the most important place to begin.

Robin is a mother of two teen boys, a former editor, a sometimes blogger and a proud introvert. She has also been an avid mussar student of mine for over a decade. Here's her reflection.

*It's hard to think of any area of my life that has **not** been enriched by the teachings of mussar. The lessons I have learned have fundamentally affected who I am today and the person I aspire to be. Opening myself up to the principles of mussar taught me quickly that the point is not to learn how to help other people in your life stretch, grow or change. Mussar is about stretching and striving to improve yourself and your behaviors.*

Complaining or venting about challenging family members is satisfying for two minutes, and then it just feels icky. After nearly 50 years of a complicated relationship with my mother, it was obvious that the only way for me to move forward and past the pain was to change my reactions and responses.

Mussar helped me understand that some things are unknowable and that giving the benefit of the doubt to others is not only charitable but helps us to refine our characters. Once I acknowledged that my mother likely had many struggles that predated me or did not involve me, I was able to soften my anger and inch ever closer to forgiveness. That is the transformative power of learning and living mussar.

CHAPTER 3: Acceptance—Accepting Others Can Be So Hard, But We Can Do It

In our chapter on judgment, we highlighted that the most advanced level of viewing others is through unconditional love. Let's explore that idea a little more deeply.

People occupy different spheres in our lives. We may love them but we don't necessarily like them all the time, and this includes family members. And we may love others but we don't act very loving towards them. That may be because they are flawed and imperfect and unlikely to change. We wish they could be different, for their own sakes. It's hard to accept these limitations in the people we love. People in other areas of our lives, such as acquaintances, neighbors, and co-workers, are people we may not love *or* like, but we must learn to co-exist with them and accept them for who they are.

Jewish mysticism teaches that the people in our lives and everything that happens to us is *bashert* (meant to be) for us. There is a plan to the universe. The people in our lives, with all their strengths and weaknesses, with all their challenges and blessings, are placed before us very specifically by a loving God. Somehow their souls and ours needed to intersect. We are the exact friends, acquaintances, and relatives whom they need in their

The people in our lives, with all their strengths and weaknesses, with all their challenges and blessings, are given specifically to us by a loving God.

lives for their souls' journeys. And they are the exact people whom our souls need (at least for a short period) in our journey as well.[1]

Many of our Biblical patriarchs and matriarchs struggled with difficult or even wicked parents, conniving siblings, enemies from other nations and from within, and/or wayward children. Abraham in particular is a shining example for us of how to approach these relationships with acceptance and kindness.

Abraham's nephew Lot, for instance, was a complex figure. On the one hand, Lot grew up in Abraham's home and absorbed the lessons of morality and hospitality modeled in that home. Despite this, Lot was tempted by the material riches available in the corrupt but wealthy land of Sodom. When Lot's life was endangered during a regional war, even though he had chosen badly and left Abraham's influence, Abraham risked his life and prepared for battle against powerful armies to save Lot. (Genesis 13-14)

But there's another relationship in Abraham's life that's even more significant, and we don't get the full story from the text alone. Rather, our traditional wisdom fills in the surprising details to which the text only alludes.

Abraham's first son, Ishmael, was caught corrupting his younger son, Isaac. Seeing this, Isaac's mother, Sarah, insisted on sending Ishmael out of the house. Although Abraham was greatly distressed, God told him to listen to Sarah. With no choice, Abraham sent Ishmael and his mother, Hagar, into the wilderness, packing along food and drinks for them. (Genesis 20)

But that's not the end of the story. What we don't see in the Biblical text but is handed down through over 3,000 years of ancient Jewish wisdom is that Abraham continued to visit his wayward son, bringing him gifts and blessings and maintaining their relationship.[2] In fact, we discover that toward the end of his life, Ishmael returns to the value system of his father.

Abraham is teaching us the lesson that you can't always make the people you love behave the way you want them to. But you can still choose to accept them, to love them, and to keep the relationship alive.

Why love doesn't come as naturally as we would like it to

In an emotionally healthy space, people are imbued with a natural affection for their parents, siblings, and offspring. We want to love and we want to be loved. Sometimes this love blinds us and we are incapable of seeing any flaws in our loved ones. This is obviously a problem. The classic mussar text *Ways of the Righteous*, mentions this problem in the chapter on "Love."[3] Most of the chapter is about loving too much, with parents being primary examples. We're all too familiar with this dynamic in our society with the spotlight on "helicopter parents" (those who hover and monitor every little detail) and "lawnmower parents" (those who clear every path for their kids).

But here I want to focus on the opposite problem: loving too little. The uncomfortable and embarrassing truth is that love often does not come naturally. Sometimes, parents and children, siblings, and friends can harbor dislike and even hatred for each other.

Sometimes the people we love embarrass and frustrate us. They don't follow our carefully laid plans. They stymie our expectations and their independent thinking may lead them to have widely divergent political and religious views from ours. The choices they make might cause them to lose their jobs or status. They may have habits we don't approve of such as smoking, drinking, interrupting, or ignoring text messages. They change over the years. And because we "care," we come down hard on them, criticize, antagonize—and alienate.

This is called *conditional love*. I will love you when you behave the way I want you to. This is not other-love, it's self-love. I love the me that I see in you.

The truth is that the best way to have the best relationships is not with external control and pressure (even disguised as "advice because I care") but rather with something else entirely. And that something is called radical acceptance.

Radical acceptance is a term I borrowed from a therapy discipline called DBT (Dialectical Behavior Therapy). It is a theory I have learned from various educators including Jewish activist Avi Fishoff of Brooklyn, New York; therapist Devorah Weiss of Edison, New Jersey; and Dr. William Glasser and his books about "Choice Theory."[4] Radical acceptance is the most unexpected way to handle people who are difficult or going through a difficult time. In my experience, it is also the most spiritual, mussar-oriented, and successful way to be in a relationship.

49

Maybe you've talked yourself blue in the face trying to convince your best friend to stop hanging out with unhealthy men. Maybe you've been begging your mother to go for therapy to process years of trauma. Maybe you can recall desperately trying to get a friend to lose weight or change his political views.

Have any of these techniques worked? Have you *ever* been successful in fixing and changing another person who does not want to be fixed or changed?

In the timeless words of author Anne Lamott, "There is almost nothing outside of you that will help in any kind of lasting way, unless you're waiting for an organ. You can't buy, achieve or date serenity and peace of mind. This is the most horrible truth, and I so resent it. But it's an inside job, and we can't arrange peace or lasting improvement for the people we love most in the world. They have to find their own ways, their own answers. You can't run alongside your grown children with sunscreen and ChapStick on their hero's journey. You have to release them. It's disrespectful not to. And if it's someone else's problem, you probably don't have the answer, anyway. Our help is usually not very helpful. Our help is often toxic. And help is the sunny side of control. Stop helping so much. Don't get your help and goodness all over everybody."[5]

Has anyone you've ever loved said, "Wow, therapy! I would never have thought of that!"

Have you ever been successful in fixing and changing another person who does not want to be fixed or changed?

"Dad, thanks for pointing out that this friend brings out the worst in me. I never noticed that before!"

"Really, the other presidential candidate has some redemptive value? I'd never considered that! Let's explore this now, you and me."

That kind of response is very rare.

Don't you think that the people in your life already know your opinions and values? Repeating facts they already know will only antagonize them and further erode the relationship. If you've already tried traditional approaches and they're failing you, it's time to try something new.

In radical acceptance we tell our loved ones in word and deed, "I love and accept you exactly as you are. I understand you. I will not judge you. I will not criticize you. I will accept your reality as you see it." It's important to note that accepting others doesn't mean we approve of their behaviors. With our love and help, with our acceptance, with spending time together in a fun and light atmosphere with no judgment, the difficult people in our lives will have the best chance of emerging from these struggles and differences healthy and emotionally safe. They will have the best chance at looking to us as their rock and support. They will be most likely to consider us and our values if and when they may seek guidance.

Acceptance is our path to learning to respect all humanity

What about all the people in our lives whom we do not love, but with whom our lives intersect all the time? This would include strangers, acquaintances, co-workers, perhaps extended family members or friends of our spouses or children. These people are also in our lives for a reason. Sometimes it's easier to accept people we barely know, but sometimes we may find it easier to judge them harshly and assume the worst because these relationships operate outside the context of love.

Judaism teaches that we should be trying to cultivate *ahavat ha-briyos*—love for all of God's creatures.[6] Every single human being is created in the image of God and has a spark of the divine within themselves.[7] Every single person has something lovable, or at least likable, about them. Can we teach ourselves to look for it? Can we teach ourselves to see it? Can we teach ourselves to identify the other by it?

Radical acceptance posits that difficult people are difficult for a reason. In the words of a famous quote, "All behavior is communication." Many people do not feel safe enough, or aren't aware enough, or aren't eloquent enough to let us know how they are feeling and why. It often comes out through academic struggles, disrespect toward authority, addictive behaviors, poor social skills, trouble with the law, anger-management issues or other behaviors. But one thing is certain. Those who behave badly have a reason, and they behave the way they do as a response or reaction to those triggers.

Those triggers could include many things. Some have a hard time learning. Others struggle socially. Some have suffered trauma or abuse, whether known or unknown to their family and friends. Sometimes the environment at home is unhealthy. Maybe there is undiagnosed mental illness.

Accepting others for who they are means behaving with kindness and respect. That's on the level of action. But in terms of thought and attitude, it means assuming the best about people, keeping all of the above in mind, and seeking ways to get along. Often, radically accepting others by telling yourself, "They're doing the best they can with their emotional abilities" (even if that turns out to be untrue), is the most peaceful and serene way to handle people, especially difficult people. So many times, radically accepting others will soften them and entice them to back down, be less harsh, and treat you with similar kindness and acceptance. In this way, the character trait of accepting others is building on the foundation we have already established, by judging favorably and practicing forgiveness.

Years ago one of our kids was in occupational therapy. He had not yet been diagnosed with ADHD, but it was presumed that were he to jump around on trampolines for an hour each Tuesday, it would help. It did not, though he certainly did enjoy it.

In any case, the receptionist at this particular office was as surly as could be. The first few times I went I was short-tempered and annoyed. *Why would this office hire a grouchy person to be a receptionist? Isn't her job to make us feel welcome?* Then I made myself a challenge: *You will make her your friend.*

First, I accepted her for who she was. To be fair, I had little to go on, but I decided that maybe she had a hard life and was doing the best she could. I memorized her name from her name tag. The next Tuesday, I started greeting her with a smile and by name. The following Tuesday, I baked her some cookies and thanked her for her service and for being there for us each week.

By the time our insurance ran out, we were buddies. She started greeting me with a smile. Radical acceptance begets radical acceptance.

God loves us unconditionally

Rabbi Akiva, a great sage and leader from 2,000 years ago, teaches that man is beloved since he is created in the image of God.[8] We are all children of God, so treating all of God's children with unconditional love, and especially His children whom He placed directly in our lives, is Godly behavior.

Many people find this very hard to grasp. They have a lot of resistance to these ideas. They don't want to let others "walk all over them."

And in truth, just as our patriarch Jacob did with his dangerous brother Esau, we sometimes have to protect ourselves from those who might hurt us.[9] Radical acceptance is an attitude in releasing pointless control and learning to love and accept the person who is before you, but as the Torah cautions, "*Chayecha kodmim*,"[10] your own life comes first. We must take the right precautions to keep ourselves healthy with healthy boundaries. Addicts may steal from loved ones and unhealthy friends can take advantage of "nice" people, crashing on their couch for weeks with no plan for the future. Be kind, but be smart.

We must not infantilize others in our desire to repair their brokenness. When we do, we are essentially telling them, "You are incapable of functioning. You have bad judgment. You cannot manage without me. Your choices, without my intervention, will probably be terrible." What kind of message is that?

Having a difficult person in your life can be traumatic no matter what. But radical acceptance creates a calm and loving atmosphere instead of one that is constantly fraught with stress and fighting.

Radical acceptance means recognizing the individual struggle of each person, and that often people are usually doing the best they can. If they could do better, they probably would do better. Why would people consciously choose to invite the wrath and disapproval of friends and relatives? Why would someone want to be depressed and risk losing everything that is precious and valuable?

Unconditional love brings the stress level way down, allowing us to leave the worrying to God. Just as God offers unconditional love to all of us, so must we offer it to others. I might have to stop lending money to my brother because I know he uses it to buy lottery tickets, but I can still love him as I protect myself from his bad behavior. I might decide to stop discussing politics with my cousin and continue to get together in ways that don't focus on our differences. I might recognize that my mother-in-law is doing the best she can, given her background, and love the lovable parts of her personality. This is called emulating God.

How acceptance helps our relationships thrive

Mussar teaches that the relationships we have are a custom-designed, divinely-orchestrated obstacle course in character refinement. The buttons our loved ones push need to be pushed. The issues they uncover must be confronted. And the blessings they carry are ours to discover—if we can only get past our own egos. So many times, the angst of loving others is our own fault because we tell ourselves the wrong story. *"I must make this work—he needs to learn—I can't let her go out like that—how dare she embarrass me."*

Repeating these messages to ourselves is a choice and a bad one. We aggravate ourselves and others, and make joy and growth impossible. And the worst part is, it doesn't even work! This approach never yields better behavior or values. Sometimes it might in the short term, but rarely in the long term. People will just learn to hide their true selves from us. We win the battle, only to lose the war.

From the mussar standpoint, external control works totally against all the positive character traits one should try to cultivate as a human being: patience, serenity, understanding, humbleness, suspension of judgment. Personally, my biggest mussar test to date has been my journey to acceptance.

In my life, my personal journey in parenting has taught me an enormous amount of acceptance. With a large family, thank God, each child is different and each has a different lesson to teach me. Any parent will agree that watching your children grow and develop into unique human beings, independent from and different from you, is one of the most astonishing things to witness. As my kids grow and find their own way, religiously and emotionally, it's almost brutal not to jump in and try to fix their mistakes. But I can't. I must accept what I cannot change. This has been a seismic shift for me personally and has impacted much of my teaching. Saying to myself, "I am not God. I cannot control the outcome," is a deeply difficult and important sentence that I have learned.

No matter what we are trying to accomplish in this world, I hope it is clear that we don't have control over the outcome. The only thing we have control over is the process. Of course, the process, done right, yields the best possible chance for a positive outcome, but that isn't the point. The point is that if we navigate the *process* correctly, we will reap the biggest spiritual, relationship, and ethical rewards.

A wise handling of the relationship journey includes putting our egos aside to truly understand others. If we can also suspend our expectations, if we become humble and generous in the journey, it will have been a success, no matter how that "success" looks on paper (or Facebook). Because if the purpose of our journey on this planet is to become more holy, more Godly people, and cultivate that holiness and Godliness in others, then it is the process that makes it a success irrespective of the final product. The success of our relationships will be in how we handle them—not in how they end up.

The words, "I am not God. I cannot control the outcome," are deeply difficult and important.

Obstacles to acceptance

Why is it so hard to accept others? Why do we try so hard to change them?

As with many traits, I think one of the biggest challenges is our own ego. If you consider my encounter with the receptionist, you'll notice that my initial reaction was quite arrogant: *How dare she! I wouldn't! I know better. I'd do better.*

Arrogance can lead us to be impatient, which is a deterrent as well. Arrogance makes it hard for us to be patient with the messiness of others. We want what we want, and we want it now! We have unrealistic expectations of others and that makes us angry and impatient when those expectations go unfulfilled. The whole notion of control is an egotistical one. We think we're God—we'll fix and change others. We'll redact the universe for our purposes, thankyouverymuch.

So to overcome these obstacles, we must release the idea of control. As the saying goes, there are only two things you need to know about religion. One, there is a God. Two, you're not Him.

We must embrace humility and patience. Remember that all this angst is here to teach us humility, to teach us patience, to help us learn to love unconditionally, to accept. Slow down the heart rate and accept the messiness that is life. It's about process, not product.

And this brings me to the most incredible and unexpected benefit of radical acceptance: the difference it will make in *you*. When you practice mussar and look at the universe through the lens of radical acceptance, whether it is looking at your own child (of any age), or any fellow human, you will realize that nearly always, people with bad or frustrating behavior are people in pain. The short-tempered cashier. The surly teen. The grouchy grandpa. The stingy uncle. The disrespectful, the rude, the angry, the anti-social. All of them are likely in pain and lack the psychological wherewithal to navigate this world on a more even keel.

When you gain this understanding and summon compassion, you will become transformed as a human being. You will discover that you are kinder and calmer. You will learn to relinquish control and stop trying to fix people. If they are broken, it is because they have been judged and hurt. The way to heal them is with love and acceptance. Your mussar journey paves the way.

You may even learn along the way to radically accept yourself.

Lisa was on an Israel trip with me in 2018 and has been listening to my mussar teachings online. She says:

I have been studying mussar for a few months now by listening to your podcast daily when I am driving to and from work.

Before studying mussar, I was very quick to "fly off the handle" and unsure of how I was going to handle issues. I am now more able to stay confident and focused when making choices and decisions, and when dealing with my daughters, who are young adults. When one of my children was having an unusually difficult time, I referenced God for the first time in my life to her, saying that I have trust in God that it would all work out. Literally, all fell into place the next day.

My life has been enriched by studying mussar. I woke up one day after listening to you for several months and realized I had changed from within. I have become more confident and am able to make rational, well thought-out decisions, and able to provide advice when it comes to discussing important topics with my daughters. As a result, my relationship with my children has strengthened by leaps and bounds and I find that they are comfortable coming to me to discuss all types of things, and we are usually on the same page with many issues. They give so much more hugging, kissing and warmth to me now, and know they can come to me with anything and I will not pass judgment.

CHAPTER 4: GENEROSITY—It's about Much More than Money

How we learn to become givers

We have arrived close to the halfway point in our exploration of the eight character traits that are the foundation of the mussar I have taught for many years. Let's take a moment to see how the traits we have discussed so far build upon one another, creating that sturdy foundation.

In Chapter 1 we discussed the benefits of offering favorable judgment, learning to give the benefit of the doubt, and learning to see situations with new eyes, which can imagine a more favorable backstory than we might first have imagined. In Chapter 2, we moved on to exploring the value of forgiveness, why it's so hard, yet also why it's so important, including the importance of forgiving ourselves. In Chapter 3, we discussed practicing acceptance—even radical acceptance—of others in our lives. This also means accepting that even difficult people in our lives are there for a purpose. Now that we are growing in our ability to incorporate these traits into our beings, we are ready for the next rung on the ladder: becoming a giver.

Jewish wisdom teaches that becoming givers is one of the important goals that we must strive toward on this planet.[1] We are all born innately selfish. Babies only think of themselves. When they're hungry they cry, and when they're tired they cry, and when they need something, yup, they cry. A toddler's favorite words are *mine* and *no*. They are realizing that there are others in this world and that the needs and desires of other people may pose a threat to their ability to get what they want. As we mature, we hope we evolve, being less self-absorbed and cultivating generosity toward others.

Usually, when we think of "generosity" we immediately think of money. But becoming a giver goes much deeper than parting with your hard-earned cash. Generosity *is* about sharing your material things. But it's also about sharing your time and your ideas. It's also about sharing your feelings, your heart, and your deepest self with another human being. And that is the most difficult form of generosity of all.

The vastness of the cosmos is unfathomable. Yet so far, intelligent life has yet to be found outside of our planet. We are all clustered onto this one huge orb, and we further cluster ourselves into countries, communities, churches, synagogues, and families. We are inexorably drawn to one another even while we sometimes repel each other. The desire and the need to connect with other people simultaneously brings us so much joy, and sometimes so much sorrow. How are we to understand this?

If you think about it, God put all humans together and created us as an interdependent system. We all have weaknesses that are filled in by each other's strengths. This allows us to become givers.

We all have weaknesses that are filled in by each other's strengths.

62

Some people look around at the people in their lives and dismiss their fellow travelers in life as random curiosities, like fellow airplane occupants. Oh, look, we both happen to be on the same flight. Guess we'll be polite to each other (or not). But, as we discussed in the last chapter, the mystical view is that each person's presence in your life is by God's design. Everyone was put into your life for a purpose. And one of the important reasons they are there is to help you become more selfless.

However, nobody said it would be easy. Every person in your life will serve you in some way—and often, those same people will also trigger you in some way.

Let's start with the people in our families of origin. Jewish philosophy encourages us to marry and create families.[2] We are meant to settle the world as God intended and enable all the other precepts of God to be fulfilled.[3] In creating families, we are charged to teach our children the values that will enable them to know how to continue the human race according to God's plan. But being part of a family is also the best way to become a giver.

It's one thing to learn how to be charitable to strangers. Ironically, it's much harder to be consistently kind and generous to the people who share your home or daily life. The people closest to us, whether we live with them or work with them, and as much as we may love them dearly, know how to push our buttons. That's exactly why these relationships are the best laboratory for learning how to give while creating emotional bonding.

When you live with other people, your home, your kitchen, and your living room have the potential to become the holiest places on earth. That's because these are the areas where generosity of spirit is most tested. This is the crucible of character. This is where you can't hide your true self. If you can prioritize emotional intimacy—being generous with your love, forgiveness, time, and trust—with those closest to you, if you can think of others and about what would make *them* feel loved and valued, raising their needs above your own, you will become a giver. And that is one of the most important goals of this life.

> *When you live with other human beings, your home, your kitchen, and your living room are the holiest places on earth.*

There are people celebrating their 10th, 25th, or even 50th wedding anniversaries who are not close at all! There are siblings who haven't spoken to each other in decades. These are sad examples of wasted time and wasted potential.

Bonding with others is a partnership

I chanced upon the work of relationship guru Mort Fertel, author of *Marriage Fitness*.[4] He speaks of a phenomenon that he calls the "communication myth." His insights are relevant not just in marriages, but in all relationships. He suggests that couples in crisis often try to mend their wounds by talking to one another about their gripes—sometimes in therapeutic environments, other times on their own. This usually doesn't solve the problem at all and even makes it worse! Why?

He describes the problem thus: imagine you have a boiler in your home and the boiler is broken. The water is not heating up, so the pipes are carrying cold water. The kitchen sink, the upstairs shower, and the dishwasher—all cold. Now imagine someone turning on the sink in his bathroom and noticing the water's cold. *The pipes!* He thinks. *We have to fix the pipes!* So he replaces all the pipes. But the water is still cold.

The water will not warm up until the boiler is fixed. If the boiler does not heat up the water, the pipes can't solve anything. The pipes are simply carrying what the boiler provides. The pipes are a conduit; they can't create something that doesn't exist.

If the feelings within the hearts of two people in a relationship are cold, the relationship is like a broken boiler. Communication can only carry to the outside what's inside. If the feelings are cold, that coldness will come out. The more that the coldness seeps out, the worse each one will feel, and the harder it will be to mend the relationship.

In my experience, good relationship therapy can be successful only when each member still has some spark of warm feelings inside—feelings that are being masked or even obliterated by the negative ones. But if all that's happening in therapy is saying things in the safety of therapy that you didn't say in private, opening the window for more frigid air to circulate, then nothing can heal. The icy mood intensifies.

In one of his emails in a series on marriage, Mort Fertel said that when you warm up the relationship from the inside, "The problems may not RESOLVE, but, even better, they will DISSOLVE." Therefore, he suggested putting the problems on a "shelf" and leaving them there while you work on warming up the boiler.

How can coldness thaw? How can disconnection—our generation's malady—heal? How can you fix the boiler?

The answer cuts to the very heart of what relationships are supposed to look like, and how Jewish wisdom suggests we get there. Spoiler: like all mussar work, it hinges on our own behaviors. Let's peek inside the Torah to discover the secret.

Genesis makes the first reference to the bonding of two human beings as one. "*Al ken ya'azov ish et aviv v'imo v'davak b'ishto v'hayu l'vasar echad.*"[5] "*Therefore, a man should leave his father and mother and cling to his wife and they shall become one flesh.*" The Hebrew verb "*v'davak*" (and cling) is telling. In modern Hebrew, the word "*devek*" means "glue." When the Torah tells us to "*davak*" to another person, it means to bond oneself to another human being.

How *do* two people become one? How do we bond? This is one of our greatest desires as human beings and one of our greatest challenges. If bonding was easy, we would not be bombarded with a thousand approaches to overcome the difficulties. Hundreds of self-help books and scores of therapists recommend different approaches to achieving this emotional bonding, leaving many of us more confused than ever. Who's right?

As a young wife, I viewed marriage as a big mystery. What was the secret? Why did some marriages succeed and others fail? How is one to make sense of all the conflicting advice about nurturing love in a marriage? My husband and I were young and in love, but that's how most marriages start. How could we beat the odds? We seemed very alike, but as our marriage progressed, our differences became more and more apparent. I'd read many marriage books, some recommended and written by Jewish mentors, and others by secular psychologists and scholars. They left me more overwhelmed than before. Maybe every book contained one nugget of wisdom, and it was my job to mine them all for the answers?

Radio personality and author Dennis Prager suggested that this transformative bonding largely boils down to luck. In one column, he wrote that sometimes we are just "lucky" enough to meet someone amazing with whom to build a beautiful life.[6] But Judaism doesn't believe in luck. Instead, it teaches us to embrace a delicate balance of God's master plan and our own human effort. Jewish wisdom teaches that success in marriage, friendship, or other relationships is a combination of God's plan and man's choice.[7]

Love is the verb that helps us gain emotional intimacy

What I've come to understand in my life from being married for over two decades, years of learning and teaching mussar, and counseling and guiding people in various relationships, is that emotional bonding must be the anchor for any relationship advice. Emotional bonding is a process fueled by determination and hard work. In other words, love is a choice. Love is also a behavior. Love is an action.

People often say, "We fell in love." "We fell out of love." "We drifted apart." "We became estranged." "We lost touch." Notice the passivity here. Our culture sends us messages that we are the hapless, passive victims of our emotions. Feelings come, feelings go. Nothing you can really do about it. Jewish wisdom radically disagrees. You are the master of your feelings. Emotional bonding results when two people make a conscious choice for closeness. We may be drawn to one another at first by chemistry (romantic or platonic) and shared values, but afterward, it is our job to actively choose to feel and understand each other's reality.

I've noticed that men in particular whose emotional needs are ignored or misunderstood will often withdraw without explanation, back off and stop trying to connect emotionally. Men generally have a harder time finding the words to express their emotional angst and often don't feel safe enough to tell others why they've retreated. Then what happens? People drift further and further away from one another emotionally until the metaphorical boiler is stone-cold.

Women, on the other hand, often take their emotional vulnerability straight to their girlfriends, who tell them exactly what they want to hear. They express their hurt feelings about their husbands, mothers-in-law, or coworkers not by trying to reconnect to those very people, but by badmouthing them to someone else who will simply agree.

In marriages, women sometimes erode emotional bonding by infantilizing their husbands to friends or relatives with comments like, "I actually have three kids: John and the girls." Since their husbands are not providing the emotional bonding they seek, these women begin to view the men as simply more "children" to look after, clean up after, and feed.

These demeaning and diminishing comments throw more buckets of ice into the rapidly cooling "boiler" in the relationship. Men might act like good sports in the moment, or they may not even hear these comments said out loud, but even if they didn't hear them explicitly, these attitudes cut very deep. Men need to feel respected by their wives more than they need to be respected by anyone else, and they need to feel respected in general a lot more than they let on.

Of course, women also need to feel respected and not diminished. Everyone needs validation and connection to feel whole, even if they may pretend they don't. This is exactly the gift of generosity that we human beings need from one another.

(I feel the need to add a caveat here. It is true that some people are simply not good partners for emotional intimacy. All the Jewish wisdom in the world cannot cure emotionally unhealthy people. While it is certainly better to see red flags and not get into relationships with those people in the first place whenever possible, sometimes, we don't have that option. If we are tied to emotionally unhealthy people, all our hard work won't solve the problem. Judaism is full of wisdom on relationships, but people who are emotionally unwell can't respond to it or practice it. Sometimes relationships do need to end or die of attrition. Our focus in this book is on those valuable relationships that suffer and end because of emotional alienation that is preventable with the right knowledge and hard work.)

Rachel's Generosity

When we say "love is a choice," or "love is a behavior," what do we mean? Jewish wisdom teaches that giving creates bonding. Rabbi Eliyahu Eliezer Dessler, a *mussar* master, Talmud scholar, and philosopher of the 20th century, explains thus:

We see that love and giving always come together. Is the giving a consequence of the love, or is perhaps the reverse true: is the love a result of the giving? We usually think it is love which causes giving because we observe that a person showers gifts and favors on the one he loves. But there is another side to the argument. Giving may bring about love for the same reason that a person loves what he himself has created or nurtured: he recognizes in it part of himself. Whether it is a child he has brought into the world, an animal he has reared, a plant he has tended, or even a thing he has made or a house he has built – a person is bound in love to the work of his hands, for in it he finds himself.[8]

In short, we bond with, even love, that in which we invest. Which means that connection often begins with acts of generosity.

When we look to our Biblical role models, we find some beautiful examples of generosity in relationships. One extremely moving example is the story of Rachel and Leah.

Rachel and Leah were sisters, the daughters of Laban, an evil and deceitful man. When Jacob arrived at their town, fleeing his evil brother Esau who wanted to kill him, he set eyes upon Rachel and immediately understood that she was his soulmate.

Asking Laban for her hand in marriage, Jacob agreed to Laban's condition that he work for him as a shepherd for seven years. The seven years flew by "out of his great love for her." And then, on the wedding night, Laban did the unthinkable. He switched his daughters, putting Leah, and in the wedding attire under the marriage canopy.[9] What a disaster!

However, traditional Jewish sources tell us that knowing Laban's propensity for deceit, Rachel and Jacob were prepared for such trickery. They had devised secret signs to transmit under the canopy to signal to one another that the right woman was marrying the right man. Yet, the wedding progressed as planned, and Jacob did not know until later that it was Leah he had wed in the ceremony. What happened to the well-laid plans?

That night, Rachel faced the most significant moral dilemma of her life. Should she let her sister be shamed under the wedding canopy in front of everyone? Or, should she share the signals with her sister, giving up the opportunity to marry the spiritual patriarch of the Jewish people, her soulmate, Jacob?

The struggle was real, and the battle tough, but in the end Rachel performed perhaps the most selfless act imaginable and shared the signs with her sister, Leah.

This act of enormous self-sacrifice came to the aid of the Jewish nation thousands of years later when they were exiled from their beloved homeland, Israel, after the destruction of the Temple. An ancient source known as the Midrash describes that, as the Babylonians ushered the Jewish captives out of their country, a conversation took place in heaven.

Each of the Patriarchs and Matriarchs came before God, recounting his or her spiritual achievements and begging God to reconsider the punishment in that merit. But it wasn't until Rachel came forth that God was moved to agree. "God," she said, "I was so selfless and not jealous of my sister and gave her the signs. I was willing to give away my husband. And you are jealous of the other gods your nation worshipped and not willing to forgive?"

God replied, "Rachel, wipe your eyes from crying, for there is reward for your efforts. Your children will be restored to their homeland!"[10]

Do we not see the truth in that prophecy today?

Rachel serves as an eternal example of generosity in relationships. One can only imagine the consequences of her actions, both familial and national, had she chosen otherwise. And while this extreme example is more valuable for its inspirational quality rather than providing one for us to emulate or even fully understand, perhaps we can ask ourselves this: How many families and communities are torn apart because someone is unwilling to even consider generosity?

"Is what I'm about to say or do going to bring us closer or further apart?"

Whereas our modern culture focuses so strongly on feelings, Jewish wisdom, as we've demonstrated, is far more concerned with behaviors. Even feelings are often malleable, a notion that modern psychology now also recognizes: fake it till you make it. The 13th-century Jewish text *Sefer HaChinuch* tells us "*Ha-adam nif'al k'fi p'ulotav*"[11]—a person is acted upon by his actions. Our external behaviors mold and shape our very internal being. We act first, and the feelings follow.

Neuroscience corroborates this. Many studies reveal that the more you behave a certain way, the more the neural pathways in your brain are altered. You literally become different! What an empowering and beautiful idea this is! We are *not* at the mercy of our personalities. We can rise above and create new habits and patterns. We are not trapped by previous choices. What this teaches us is that we should *act* in a bonding and giving way *even when* (or especially when) we don't feel like bonding or giving, because that is exactly how we can heal emotional estrangement or emotional neutrality and blossom into emotional bonding.

Dr. William Glasser, a psychologist who developed the Choice Theory method, alludes to this when he recommends that before you act, you ask yourself, "Is what I'm about to say or do going to bring us closer or further apart?"[12]

Every action we take will either bring us closer to our goal of emotional bonding—or create more walls. Every encounter is an opportunity to either heat the boiler or cool it off. It's scary to think about this, but there really is no neutral.

I almost don't want actions to matter as much as they do. Many times people will promise one another that they will come home on time, watch their spending, clean up, call more often, be more responsible, criticize less. But the promises remain empty. Aside from the estrangement that naturally follows when someone doesn't take the actions necessary for bonding, we now have the added problems of eroded trust. When it comes to emotional bonding, what you *do* is a lot more important than what you say. The reason "actions speak louder than words" became a cliché is because it's true. *Ethics of the Fathers* reminds us, "It is not the study that is the main thing, but the actions."[13]

When I help without being asked, when I show up for my friend, when I make time to be an active listener without being begged, when I notice my husband's favorite things at the grocery store and buy them just to please him, I am choosing generosity to further build our emotional intimacy. Don't just say, *do.* The Torah warns us against overcommitting and underdelivering, instead encouraging us to "say little and do much."[14] We all know people who are full of good intentions and grandiose dreams, but emotional closeness is built on reliable behaviors. We must become trustworthy. Being a steady and responsible spouse, friend, child, parent, employee, or neighbor may not seem very exciting or glamorous, but in the long haul it is exactly what endears people to one another.

What's your love language?

Every person has his own love language, though many people "speak" more than one. Dr. Gary Chapman, in his bestselling book *The 5 Love Languages*,[15] lists five "languages" that reveal the specific ways that people want to receive love. Some people appreciate affectionate touch. Others, "acts of service" such as washing the car, grocery shopping, or cleaning up (my personal favorites). Still others like to hear words of affirmation. For others, it's enjoying the gift of quality time. And some feel the love mostly through gifts. Ancient Jewish wisdom reminds us that just as no two faces are exactly alike, no two humans have exactly the same opinions and preferences.[16]

Get to know your people's love language so that when you act, you do so in a way that is other-focused and generous. It's natural for us to give love in the same way we want to receive love, without noticing whether the recipient is gratified by our "language." Read Chapman's book with your spouse or another beloved person in your life and see if you are speaking the same language after all. Maybe your "love language" isn't in the book. If not, add it yourself. Tell your parent, child, sibling, spouse, or friend what your love language is, and then listen carefully to theirs. Taking the time to understand others in a deep way is one of the greatest, most generous gifts of love you can give. Nothing builds emotional intimacy quite like that.

Obstacles to intimacy

There are many barriers that interfere with truly connecting with another human being and cultivating emotional intimacy. In mussar mode, we strive to identify the character trait (or traits) that block the path of bonding. For some, it's impatience: *I just don't have the patience to deal with this.* For others, arrogance: *I shouldn't have to deal with this! This is way worse than what I bring to the table!* Sometimes laziness deters the work: *I have no energy to deal with this.* Mort Fertel suggests that efficiency is one barrier to intimacy. This really resonates with me because (deep breath), like being judgmental, it's a weakness of mine.

Prioritizing intimacy over efficiency is very difficult for those of us with Type A personalities. If I had to determine which character trait this was, I'd identify the one called in Hebrew "*zerizut*"—industriousness. Normally *zerizut* encompasses being punctual, efficient, energetic. It's pretty much the opposite of laziness and procrastination and is usually considered a positive attribute. Our culture certainly prizes efficiency, constantly creating new technologies, apps and systems to make as much of our lives as efficient as possible.

However, in Judaism we believe that character traits are inherently *neutral.* No trait is all bad or good. Every single trait is on a continuum and can become radicalized and brought to an unhealthy extreme in either direction. Every single character trait can be used either for the good or for the bad.

For instance, kindness is good, but extended to evil or manipulative people, it is bad. Too much kindness can cripple and weaken recipients. An excessive need to be kind can also indicate an unhealthy need to be needed, leading to co-dependence and lack of healthy boundaries.

You can be generous to a fault. You can also be brutally truthful and hurt others, even though honesty is generally valued. Alternatively, you can use the "bad" trait of brashness in a positive way, to speak up boldly when leadership or courage is required. Every single trait has its time and place; each has its positive applications and its negative applications, like ingredients in a recipe. *Zerizut,* industriousness, is usually tasty, but misapplied, leaves a sour taste.

People who excel at *zerizut* are usually admired for being reliable, responsible, and efficient. But people like this— people like me—are at high risk for prioritizing efficiency over intimacy.

Here's an example from my real life.

I am in my kitchen loading my dishwasher. Now I'm sure you all know that there is a right way and a wrong way to load a dishwasher. The right way is to load smaller things on top, larger things on bottom. Small plates in front of larger ones. Knives and fork tines must always face up. Yes, even if someone will get stabbed. And obviously, *no "nesting."* Now my dear husband walks in the kitchen and starts "helping." The knot in my stomach starts to form because my "helpful" loved one is literally destroying my perfectly planned dish placement. He's doing it wrong. I'm annoyed. Doesn't he have things to do, people to see, phone calls to return?

Why is he loading the dishwasher with me? Because he's trying to connect with me and help me. He's speaking his "love language" of acts of service, so he's hanging out here in the kitchen. Through this act of generosity, he wants to lighten my (dishwashing) load and create emotional intimacy.

Why don't I like it? Because I'm consumed with efficiency. I just want to get the job done, and I want to get it done right—my way. His quest for intimacy is encroaching on my quest for efficiency. Maybe my body language or passive-aggressive comments ("Glasses don't go there") telegraph my displeasure. Maybe I even ask him to stop. I'm killing the intimacy with my hyper-focus on efficiency. I am not choosing generosity.

To be fair, it is very difficult for someone like me, who has "systems" to do things, to stop in the middle of an especially efficient moment. It is even harder to detect that the person messing with that moment is seeking emotional closeness. And most of all, it's very hard to switch gears and allow myself to slow down for the sake of nurturing intimacy with my husband. But I've learned the hard way that this gift, this generosity, is vital for a relationship.

Jewish wisdom teaches that the harder a choice is, the greater the spiritual reward.[17] Every time we master ourselves and rise above our default reaction and act nobly, we are rewarded commensurate with the effort involved. The opportunity for growth follows the difficult moments. We can acknowledge that it is difficult to overcome a character trait that works against us. But it is the focus of our spiritual work to continue to wage that battle, turning weaknesses into strengths. We may wage that battle only in small moments, tiny increments of progress, but those are likely to become the most rewarding moments in our lives.

My efficiency is part of who I am. It's what makes me, me. It's also what helps me to effectively juggle all my balls and accomplish a lot in a short amount of time. It's a gift, and I'm so grateful for it! But every character trait has its merits and demerits. Each can be used for good or for bad. It's up to us to be the masters of our traits and channel them properly. One of the dark sides of efficiency is its potential toll on relationships. Every time I squelch my need to rush out of the house for an appointment, which I will probably be early for anyway, and forcibly slow down and savor my family for another few minutes, I have taken another step toward my transformation into a kinder person. I have ceded my need to be efficient and given my loved ones the gift of closeness. I have demonstrably enhanced the bond between us. God has given me these tendencies for a reason, to teach me where my spiritual work is. When I do the work, I float through my day, knowing that I've climbed my own spiritual Everest.

Generosity also involves sharing our true emotional needs and desires

People generally do not say what they really mean when they're seeking intimacy. A woman I'll call Sandy might be feeling shut out of her brother and sister-in-law's life, and wonder if there is a reason that she is not connecting with them. What she is really feeling is, "I desire more intimacy with my brother and his family." But Sandy is far more likely to say instead, "Hey, what are you guys doing for Thanksgiving this year?"

Her brother may respond, "I don't know yet. We might go to Lisa's family. How about you?"

She then feels miffed that he took her question at face value. Sandy feels left out, because her brother didn't intuit her bid for intimacy. He answered the question the way anybody would who isn't a mind-reader.

What if Sandy allowed herself to be open and vulnerable? What if she were generous in sharing her true feelings, awkward and scary though that may be?

What if she said instead, "Hey, I'm feeling kind of disconnected from you lately, and I miss you. I would love to spend Thanksgiving together. Can you make that work?"

I don't know what will happen, but I do know this: intimacy won't create itself. Not only do we build intimacy by becoming more generous in giving of ourselves to others, but we also build it by sharing more generously our own thoughts and feelings, instead of protecting ourselves with non-conversations.

We don't necessarily need emotional intimacy with outer circles of acquaintances, but we do need some form of connection and validation. For example, at work, it can be hard for me to include the thoughts and opinions of my staff or committee members when I have a clear and sharp vision of what I want to do and how I want to do it. But I love the people I work with, and even if I didn't, I still want to have a collegial relationship with them and create a positive and nurturing environment in my organization. Most importantly, I want the workplace to be a place where we can nurture our souls and grow, as opposed to it being a soul-killing place that is the opposite of everything I stand for.

When we make ourselves human and vulnerable at work, and with extended family members or neighbors, we set the stage for connection and bonding in a way that validates others and expands our own capacity for giving and connection.

The truth is that requests for emotional intimacy, in all our various relationships, are never straightforward. We have to have our hearts wide open and our radars on so we can detect the signals when they flash. Requests for emotional intimacy often masquerade as direct questions that can be efficiently answered. Here are a few examples:

Wife: "Do you want to go out for dinner?"
Translation: I want to be with you and get dressed up and feel special and loved.
Husband: "Nah, I have too much to do."

Employee: "Hey, did you take a look at the report I left on your desk?"
Translation: I want to be validated and appreciated. I want to matter to this company. Your approval means a lot to me.
Employer: "I'll get to it. Now hurry up and get on the project we discussed yesterday."

Neighbor: "I love how your garden turned out this season! It's beautiful!"
Translation: I want to connect to you, instead of being two ships that pass in the night. I want to belong to this community.
Neighbor #2: "Yuck, nothing turned out the way I wanted."

Asking for emotional closeness makes us vulnerable. The more times you're shot down or misunderstood, the less likely you'll be to ask for it again. The more times your prioritize efficiency over intimacy, the more elusive emotional intimacy will become.

When I prioritize emotional intimacy over efficiency, I am helping to forge a closer bond with my loved one, so that two souls can become one. As Judaism teaches, we learn to "heat the boiler" so that the water that runs is warm and nurturing. If we are feeling distanced, or there is a rift, instead of talking about the rift we just need to act, to do something connective and bond-strengthening. I know: why would you want to do something nice for someone when you feel estranged from them? As my kids sometimes say, "I'm not feelin' it." If I'm not feeling the feeling, the reasoning goes, I won't act the action. But as we have explored, that is exactly the time to act. Remember, we can and often should "fake it till we make it."

I've used my own weakness of prioritizing efficiency over bonding as an example here, but maybe you are more laid back and can't relate to my example. Go back and read this chapter again, substituting your own weakness for mine: quickness to anger, laziness, over-sensitivity or under-sensitivity—whatever fits in your case. Find whatever is stopping you from bonding with the important (and minor) people in your life and work on changing. Figure out what gift of generosity you need to give in order to warm the boiler, deepen your relationships, and further your personal transformation.

My friend Shari is the mother of two young-adult men, one of whom has autism. She is also a teacher, tutor, and special needs advocate and volunteer. She has been studying mussar with me for two decades and says:

Mussar has totally changed my life. I've been learning mussar for 22 years, and whatever I'm learning is exactly what I need to hear. Learning never ends. There's nothing in my life that hasn't changed by studying mussar, because everything changes when you have your mussar eyeglasses on. Sometimes I forget and sometimes I misstep, but I always have my glasses. The older I get, the more I want to be my best self, because we never know how much time we have.

My extended family is all over the place in terms of Jewish identity and observance, and I can't change how anyone lives their life. But I can change my own learning and habits, and as I age, that's my mantra. That's my gift that I can give others.

Shari had more to say.

I heard a great quote the other day: "Unless he's wearing a diaper, you can't change him." I love my husband, but there's always ups and downs in marriage. One of our kids was struggling a lot and needed my help to get centered. My husband is more of a "pull him up by the bootstraps" kind of guy. But by me exuding generosity of spirit toward my husband and speaking kindly and calmly, I reminded him, "We really need to be united in this. Honey, he's drowning, and we have to focus on that." Because I was kind and calm, and used all my mussar tools, he was able to hear me. As a team, we could help our son.

Mussar has made my life fuller, bigger, better, and brighter. Everything is more Technicolor. The joy, the gratitude, which is where I naturally go, has been enhanced exponentially, even when I'm having a bad day. Within the struggle, I can find something to be joyful about. Also, I have really learned to let go of control. I have been trying to control things since I was a little girl, and mussar has really helped me let go of control in my life and relationships. The only one I can control is myself.

CHAPTER 5: SPEECH—Creating Reality with Our Words

We now understand very clearly that actions often speak louder than words. However, speech is also incredibly important, and it helps determine the quality of our character. In this chapter we'll unpack how powerful speech can be, and how we can work on our power of speech to make ourselves and this world a better place.

If we want to improve our interactions with the world around us, speech is a logical starting point. Life is busy and stressful, which can work against our ability to both act and speak with sensitivity and care. Personally, I know that I get "hangry" and crabby and sometimes take it out on others. Work demands, self-esteem issues, sensitivities, health or financial concerns, and lots of annoying people can all distract us from our goal of nurturing relationships, which then can fade into the background. In an unguarded moment, we lash out. We criticize and castigate, not really meaning it as a true and full expression of our personalities. In our minds, these negative encounters are just a blip on the loving horizon. Tomorrow, I'll be nicer.

As we discussed in the last chapter, the people we take our frustrations out on are, ironically, usually the people we care about most. Those are the people we feel safest with. They won't stop loving us. We have faith that they'll forgive us. This is why kids often act the worst with their own parents but may be angels at school (I'll take it, thanks). It's why we often yell at family members instead of at our bosses or even strangers. Strangely, it should be taken as a great compliment if you are someone else's punching bag.

Our loved ones don't necessarily take it that way. We can be quick to forget our critical and angry words and forgive ourselves. But while we're ready to move on, the other person is still nursing wounds. Our loved one may be deeply hurt, or even traumatized by the mean things we've said in a weak moment. In the worst case, we might damage relationships for good. Whoever said, "Sticks and stones can break my bones but words can never hurt me" was delusional. Physical pain heals far faster than emotional pain.

Jewish wisdom bears this out. The Torah has long maintained that words matter. What we say, and what we don't say, has huge import.

The Torah enumerates 613 commandments that Jews are supposed to follow. Of those, just over half are still relevant in contemporary times. (Many deal with the Temple service in the Land of Israel—the last Jewish Temple was destroyed by the Romans in 70 AD.) And of the 369 commandments relevant today, about 10% deal with how we should talk to and about one another. That's significant and speaks to the underlying principle that words matter.

So much of our contemporary society involves language in all its forms: written, spoken, emailed, texted and tweeted. Thousands of years before Twitter, the Torah referenced birds being "chatterers and twitterers" and birds were used as part of the Temple service rituals to remind us to watch our speech.[1]

Sometimes we can tell what a person is really like, such as when celebrities, politicians, or athletes are caught on a "hot mic" and their carefully polished image peels away to reveal ugly hate speech or bigotry. Their so-called apologies teach us a lot about what our society thinks about words misspoken: *"I'm sorry if you were offended… It was an indiscretion… This does not reflect how I really feel…."* If you recall from our chapter on forgiveness, these weak statements are not so much apologies as they are attempts to evade responsibility. Instead, true remorse would include an admission of guilt, along with a resolution for better choices in the future. For example: "I'm sorry that I spoke crudely and hurt people with my statements. I am committed to being more sensitive and kind in the future, and to use my words to build, not to harm."

On the other hand, society can "cancel" a person for the slightest whiff of verbal indiscretions, and an unfortunate turn of phrase can be enough to invite complete censure and destruction, especially on social media. Most of us speak, tweet, or text without planning every phrase, and sometimes wish we could pull back our words. Too often, that option is no longer offered today. The power of social media to shame or even cancel someone who has "misspoken" has made millions of people think twice before speaking or posting their thoughts or opinions. Forgiveness, even to a sincere apology, is rarely bestowed in today's society. This is not a positive trend.

As a public social media user and blogger, I have deeply regretted certain things I've written. As soon as someone starts telling me, "I remember once you said…" I get a pit in my stomach. What did I say? Should I have said it? Do I still believe that? Did it come out right? Will I have to apologize?

The words we speak are deeply important. They can wreak incredible damage or they can build human beings. Dismissing hurtful words as "just words" or excusing a rude person by saying, "Oh, that's just how he communicates" is absolutely antithetical to spiritual evolution. We human beings are the only species that communicates with intelligent, complex speech. This is both a privilege and a responsibility.

In Judaism we create reality with our words. In fact, the Hebrew word for "word" is *davar*, meaning both "word" and "thing." Words create real things. For example we welcome the Sabbath and holidays with words of blessing over candles and wine. We conclude the Sabbath and holidays with the *havdalah* ceremony, in which we verbally create a boundary between holy days and mundane days. We create marriages with words and we end them with words. We bless our food before we eat and offer verbal thanks when we're done. A person who takes a verbal vow creates a brand-new reality, and a verbal agreement in business is akin to a binding promise. Our ability to speak and to use words to create worlds is astonishing.

Let me share a life-changing example from my own life.

"I love you more than a suitcase"

I once attended a parenting seminar in New York for parents of teens. During the program, the facilitator displayed a slideshow of parents dealing with an out-of-control teen. The teen had borrowed his parents' car without permission and got into an accident. The parents sent the following text to their son: "We love you more than a car!"

What an astounding thing to say in a moment of utter fear and fury.

What was the meta-message? A child who crashes his parents' car knows he has done something serious. He doesn't actually need his parents to clue him in on this fact. Not now, not in this moment.

There is a time for conversations about responsibility and safety. But in this moment, by using powerful words to respond with love, the child recognizes something crucial: no matter how bad this is, my parents' love is bigger.

When I saw this text on the screen, my eyes filled with tears. Isn't this what we all want in life? Soul-affirming words that someone loves us so much, so unconditionally, that even when we mess up royally, we come out okay? Is this not the love God feels for us, no matter how badly we behave? Is this not the essential craving of every human being, to be loved, valued, and cherished, no matter what? To feel that there is nothing we can say or do that will make us unloved or unwanted? And all from a few words in a text message. We can give this to others! I resolved to put this into practice as soon as possible.

When my husband and I were on a trip to New York, our little daughter Nomi slept over at my sister's house. When we all came home, she forgot her suitcase there.

My husband is on the spontaneous and impulsive side, while I'm a little more staid and structured. God's sense of humor, for sure. So when my husband said he'd really rather not pick up the suitcase that day because he was tired from traveling and didn't want to make a stop, I was all amazing and said, "That's okay honey, you'll be back there tomorrow so you can just get it then," though I was secretly thinking, "Wow, that's a really bad idea, because you will probably forget."

Tomorrow came and went and no suitcase. I peeked in the hall to be sure, and yeah, no suitcase. "So," I said, "this is why I really wanted you to get it yesterday when we all remembered. Her stuff is in there and I need to wash it and blah blah blah." He apologized, I sighed loudly and we all moved on.

He went to give my daughter a bath when it hit me: was that really what I wanted to say? Were those the best words I could have chosen just then? Was it going to bring the suitcase any sooner? Was I giving him any information he didn't already have? Do I love my husband more than a car, or in our situation, a suitcase? I did. But my words had not backed that up. Although I didn't say anything terrible or hurtful, I totally missed an opportunity to bring us closer. I was overcome with a sense of regret.

I ran down the hall to the bathroom, flung open the door, and said, "Here's what I really meant to say! I LOVE YOU MORE THAN A SUITCASE!" He looked up, surprised, and we both started laughing, remembering the slideshow with the car. The tension had evaporated.

He was touched that I was trying. I resolved to get better at it so that next time, I wouldn't have to remember after the fact.

Of course, we should continue to have honest conversations with our spouses and loved ones about our needs and wants. We can discuss household maintenance, not procrastinating when asked to do things, and respecting our wishes even when inconvenient.

We can share our feelings in a loving way. But in a moment when we may be angry, we still can choose to say things that will make the other person feel okay about how they may have disappointed us. In the moment, we can say, "My love for you is bigger than any mistake." And afterwards we can have the important conversations about next time. That is what self-transformation looks like.

There have been so many times in my professional life when I have become irritated at others, assumed the worst, and shot off an email while upset and angry. I've ALWAYS regretted these communications later. As we explored in Chapter 1, assuming the best about people while waiting to react (even more on that in our next chapter) is rarely the wrong choice. Expressing our appreciation to them, even while waiting for clarity on what happened, will always be worth it.

In the moment, we can say, "My love for you is bigger than any mistake."

In our home we participate in a quirky Jewish custom. When a glass bowl or dish shatters, we all yell

"Mazal tov!" It means, "Congratulations!" At a Jewish wedding, there's a custom to break a glass under the *chuppah* (the marriage canopy) at the very end of the ceremony. This reminds us, at our greatest moment of joy, that God's Temple has not been rebuilt yet and so absolute joy isn't possible. As soon as the glass is broken, the ceremony is over, and everyone yells, "Mazal tov!" So we have come to associate breaking glass with shouting, "Congratulations!" Used in our daily lives when accidents happen, that one word breaks the tension and everyone remembers: people are more valuable than stuff.

Letting people know that they are valued

I have also come to recognize how important it is to follow through when I am appreciative of someone's actions, letting them know that I value them. Putting thought into *how* to do that adds a bonus touch.

One summer, my daughter was in a day camp in my neighborhood run by a local mom. My girl was having a great time, and I was impressed with how much care and devotion the mom put into her business. My inclination was to mention this at pickup. I was there, she was there, and I was seeing her anyway.

But then I thought about it. There was no comparison between saying something just because I happened to see this woman, and making a dedicated phone call, taking the time and forethought to reach out. So I decided to wait until Friday, the end of the week.

I picked up the phone and called her. I told her how much my daughter was enjoying camp and how I noticed how much she had put into it; that the kids and us appreciated that she was doing a really great job; that I was grateful for her devotion.

There was a pregnant pause, then elation.

"Ruchi," she said, "you literally made my day. No, my week! No, you made this camp worth running! Thank you! Thank you for noticing, and thank you for calling."

This mom friend of mine went on to expand her camp the following year. Over the years, she has incorporated her camp, rented space in a school building, hired staff, done an incredible marketing job, and essentially launched her own small business.

I'm glad I noticed and called her when she ran a little camp in her backyard. And while I'm not arrogant enough to think my little phone call sparked that confidence, I do know one thing: it felt significant.

Validation means understanding, not fixing

Using words for the good also means we can use them to validate others. Validation is the kind of feeling that when feel deprived of it, you're fuming, and when you do get it, you feel instant relief. It is a minor shift with major impact. With a few carefully chosen words, you can instantly boost a person's emotional state.

What am I talking about?

When people share their woes with me, either major or minor, they want one of two things. Either they want me to save, solve and fix; or they want me to share, care, and encourage.

Let's say a friend confides in me and says, "Ugh, Ruchi, I'm feeling so fat." My instinct is to say, "No, you're not!" What have I just done? I have effectively told her that her feelings are invalid. Or I might say, "Hey, come to the gym with me!" Is that better? Meh. Telling her this is my way of solving the issue. In this mode, I'm trying to save her from her negative feelings. It's another way where I am trying to fix the problem.

But what if I tried something else? What if instead of trying to save or fix, I simply used my words to be with my friend in her pain? What if I didn't try to change anything? (It's hard to think this way, especially for a fixer like me.) So when my friend says, "I feel fat," I could simply say, "Oh, I know how that feels. It's a yucky feeling." Or, "Ugh, I've had those days. I'm sorry."

When I remember to *share, care and encourage*, the other person doesn't feel invalidated but understood instead. In my experience, most people usually want for me to share, care, and encourage. So why is my primal instinct always to save, solve and fix?

It feels like a good deed to fix another person's problems. It seems like a spiritual act of kindness. But maybe it's not.

God Himself reassures us in Psalm 91, "I am with him in his pain."[2] God is with us when we suffer, and that's why

94

He appeared to Moses in a burning bush. If the Children of Israel are in the inferno of Egypt, then I too, says God, am in an inferno with them. Moses demonstrates the very same trait when he is raised in Pharaoh's palace, immune to the Egyptian oppression, yet he goes out regularly to his brothers to be with them in their suffering. It's not about fixing, but about simply being with someone in their pain, with no judgment or Superman cape that eases their burden.

I once got a speeding ticket, and I came home grouchy and annoyed—mostly at myself.

Here's what my husband might have said, listed here from worst to best:

Dismissal: "What on earth? Can't you be more careful? What a waste of money!"

Save, solve and fix: "OK, give it to me and I'll take care of it. Be more careful next time so this doesn't happen again."

Share, care and encourage: "Oh, honey. That is so upsetting. I just hate when those kinds of things happen to me. Sit down and let me make you some tea."

It's amazing how the third statement does nothing to solve the problem but feels the best. Helping another person feel understood and meeting them where they are emotionally is one of the greatest acts of kindness. Overcoming our temptation to fix things helps us in our interactions with anyone we meet and fosters our growth as human beings.

When teaching a group of teens in our congregation, I tried a little experiment. I asked the girls in the group, "If you had a really bad day, and you told a group of girlfriends that you had a bad day, what would be the likely response?" They all answered that their girlfriends would be likely to give a hug and say things like, "I'm sorry," "I hope tomorrow is better," "I understand." These words encourage and care. They do not fix anything, but the girls reported instantly feeling better when they heard these words.

Then I asked the guys in the group the same question, but with them asking their guy friends. What did the guys predict their friends would say? They said: "Suck it up, dude." "We all have bad days; deal with it." In other words, something between dismissal and fixing. Or maybe trying to fix by dismissing. It was a revealing experiment, and both groups thought carefully about the impact of validating words.

Even when we understand how powerful this idea is of offering simple caring and sharing, it can be hard to stop "fixing," at least for me. After one lecture I had given in Providence, Rhode Island on the topic of validation, a woman came over after my talk and asked if we could take a selfie. I said sure, and she snapped the photo. Of course we both inspected her phone afterwards to assess the photo's shareability. She said, "Oh, I look terrible." Immediately, without even blinking, I said, "No, you look great!"

She looked me full in the face and said, "Didn't you just finish teaching us about validation?" We both laughed and laughed. It is so ingrained in us to deflect uncomfortable feelings! I apologized and said instead, "I'm sorry you're unhappy with how you came out. Should we take it again?"

Why are we so drawn to fixing other people's problems instead of validating them? What's the obstacle to using our words more helpfully?

I think it comes from something I'll call "selfish empathy." When people I care about complain to me, I become uncomfortable because I feel their pain. Since I love them, I want to move them and myself away from that pain by trying to swat it away like an annoying mosquito. And since I'm a fixer, it seems natural to move into fixer mode. By explaining away the pain, maybe I can save them— and myself—from discomfort.

But the truth is different. Explaining away pain may make *me* feel better, and even like a hero, but it does nothing for the other person. In fact, he or she may feel misunderstood, dismissed, invalidated, lonelier than before, and less likely to share with us in the future.

One of the character traits we are to aspire to in Judaism is called *nosei b'ol im chaveiro*, "bearing the burden with your friend." The Torah is full of examples where great leaders were with their flock in their pain.

Moses was chosen as the leader of the Jewish people for just this reason. As noted, though he was raised in Pharaoh's palace, he went out from that privileged space to see his brothers' pain. Later, when a small sheep ran away from his flock, Moses lovingly and carefully carried it back, offering words of empathy as opposed to annoyance.[3]

Notice the preposition used in the character trait: bearing the burden *with* your friend. Not *instead*. Not *pushing away the burden* or *explaining it away*. Simply being there together, avoiding unhelpful words in favor of validating and loving ones. Selflessly being willing to get down in the hole with your friend so that you are in that dark place together.

Researcher Brene Brown talks about this idea in a short animated YouTube video about the difference between sympathy and empathy.[4] When someone falls into a dark hole, you can either yell down, "Hey! Are you all right?" and throw down a sandwich (save, solve and fix), or climb down into the hole and just sit together, saying, "I'm here with you. It's okay to be sad." Now *that's* how you share, care and encourage. And by shifting our words even in these small ways, we make a big booming difference in our families and communities.

Are we criticizing out of concern or out of self-interest?

Another way to use our speech more constructively is when we need to deliver feedback to others. There are ways to do this that build others up and cultivate kindness within ourselves, and there are ways to do this that tear others down and make us more cruel and callous.

I'm a firm believer that almost anything can be said as long as it's said in the right way, but the technique takes practice. For some, the practice is to temper harsh criticism and deliver it in a kinder, more constructive way. For others, the challenge is to learn to speak up at all and summon the courage to say what needs to be said.

How can the Torah's wisdom guide us here?

There is a mitzvah to rebuke one's fellow and help him become his best self: "Do not hate your brother in your heart; you shall surely rebuke him and not incur guilt because of him."[5]

After all our talk about offering validation and empathy, how can we understand this directive? First, this is a clear instruction that sometimes it is incumbent on us to give others constructive criticism. I like to joke that there are 3½ categories of people whom we can tell off. Everyone usually guesses their spouse first. But no. The three categories are: one's child, one's student, and one's employee. These three categories of people need and rely on your guidance to become the people they are meant to become. And the half is your spouse, because spouses are supposed to lovingly bring out the best in each other. It goes both ways of course. With spouses, we must be open to getting as well as giving constructive feedback.

As an employer, I sometimes have to do this at work. As a parent, it comes up plenty. As a teacher, it's my job. In these arenas it's a responsibility, and I would be careless to shirk it. You probably have your own areas where you have the same obligations. Now, some people love criticizing, but for those of us who are people pleasers, we'd often rather say nothing than confront an issue that needs to be addressed.

But this verse started with an intriguing statement, that we should not hate someone in our heart. If we have a problem with someone, we need to carefully talk it out and clear the air. It is dangerous to harbor negative attitudes and to feel virtuous while withholding the opportunity for the other person to voice their side of the story. Bottled up feelings inevitably will build up and explode. The remedy is to speak things out and tell the person what is on your mind. The result is that the "hatred in the heart" will diffuse, making way for mutual understanding and renewed connection.

But now let's get to the meat and potatoes of this instruction. How *do* we rebuke another person so that we don't inflame the negative feelings, and in a way that does not pile on more mistakes? How do we make sure we won't make everything worse?

Jewish wisdom offers clear guidelines.[6] First, the rebuke must be offered for the well-being of the other person. If you're shooting off your mouth to satisfy your own judgmentalism or aggravation, that is selfish and not constructive. You must make every effort to ensure that the other person senses that your intention is for his or her well-being. If that feeling of authentic concern is not there, your words will not be accepted. This is too important a conversation to have via texting. Meet in person if at all possible. Speak in private, never in front of others. Communicate with care and dignity. If you are not confident that the circumstances are in place to have a successful conversation, don't have it.

My neighbors were doing construction and there was a "Porta Potty" on the front lawn for the workers. Every time I walked by, I smelled it. I considered asking them to move it to the backyard, but wondered if I should say anything. My first thought was, this is temporary. Is it really that upsetting? Can't I just let it go? This is not about helping my friend live a better life; it's purely for my benefit. If I were in true distress, I could certainly still say something to my neighbor, even if it were for my benefit, but all the rules would still apply. I'd need to speak kindly, privately, and with regard for my neighbor's dignity. In the end, I did choose to let it go. I reframed it as an active, conscious, noble act, as opposed to the view that cast me as victim. It felt liberating. It felt great. It doesn't, actually, always pay to "let it all out."

Let's use a trickier example. Let's say I see a friend of mine adopting some troubling habits, even engaging in harmful relationships or addictive behaviors. I hurt for her. I am worried about her. I want to help her. What should I do?

Again, some of us lean too heavily toward always telling others what to do and consistently offering unsolicited advice. But some of us lean too heavily the other way. We never want to rock the boat or risk making others mad. Neither of these extremes serve us.

I'm so allergic to unsolicited advice that I will rarely tell others what to do, even when I should. For me, offering constructive criticism is hard to do (except to my husband and children). Frankly, I hate when people tell me what to do. I even say, when venting to a friend, "Just sympathy, no advice, please." But there are times when playing it safe is dangerous.

I should have a conversation with my fictional friend who is exhibiting worrisome signs. I should invite her to talk in person, or if that's impossible, on the phone. She needs to feel that my entire focus is on her well-being, not my fear or worry. I should offer her dignity and assume the best about her and validate her. But I should tell her I am concerned. I should tell her I am there for her. I should ask her how I can be helpful. And then, I should stop talking and just listen.

The struggle between saying too much and saying too little is real. It's a tightrope—say too much and you've alienated the other person. Your words and wisdom will have zero impact. Say too little, and you've shirked your responsibility to your friend. This is so tricky that some Jewish authorities assert that no one actually knows how to deliver rebuke appropriately nowadays, and therefore no one should try it.[7] Nonetheless, there are times that not saying anything is just the wrong thing. It means not being a good friend. And even leaving friends aside, we are still responsible for 3½ categories of people: our children, our students, our employees, and our spouses.

The struggle between saying too much and saying too little is real.

When I was in middle school, there was a student in our class who had special needs. I thought we were all being nice to her and inclusive, but she was unhappy. To be fair, young adolescents are ill-equipped to handle delicate social situations well, especially where there is a special need or circumstance. To be even more fair, I don't think our school was the right fit for this girl. In any case, our principal came into our classroom one day when this new girl was out and gave us a little rebuke. I remember what she said word for word as if it was yesterday.

"Girls, it seems that X is not happy here in our school. And I am putting most of the blame on you girls."

What I remember most is that this rebuke was not delivered in an angry or accusatory way. It did not leave me feeling defensive or misunderstood. Instead, I felt that the rebuke enhanced my awareness of how to treat a newcomer. Our principal was calm and kind. She just said what needed to be said. Regardless of our principal's efforts, the girl eventually switched to another school.

From my adult vantage point, looking back I actually don't think that "most of the blame" was on us girls, but that's not really the point. The point is that I saw a true role modeling of what proper rebuke looks like. It consists of kind, caring, teachable moments that leave the other party feeling respected, with a renewed desire to do better.

Words of criticism, whether given or received, are powerful, and we underestimate their power. I also think that we frequently speak reactively, without really asking ourselves some important questions first. If we are tempted to react to words spoken to us, do we first ask ourselves: *Who said it? What did they say? Why did they say it? What did they mean? Is it true? What can I learn from it? Should I say something?*

And, if we want to say something, do we first ask ourselves: *Why am I saying it? To whom should it be said? When, where, and how? What is my intent? What is the likely outcome?*

Criticism is a sharp tool. It can hurt and it can repair. It's up to us to determine how we will send out our powerful words into the universe, and it is up to us to determine how we will receive them when they come our way.

Critiques can help us grow, if we let them

Now that we've explored the words we say or don't say about others, we are ready to discuss the other side of the coin: words spoken about you or to you.

"Feedback" is a big buzzword in business today. We're bombarded with online surveys, because every company and organization worth its salt solicits feedback. Why? Because they want to improve.

As a co-founder and associate director of our own congregation, my husband and I are also solicitors of feedback. We solicit in person, at board meetings, via email, and online after big events such as High Holiday services and weekend retreats. I can tell you from experience how it feels to read various types of feedback.

The compliments are really fun to read. We run a small local operation so we know everyone personally, and it's so enjoyable to read the high ratings and effusive compliments expressing the joy that others have derived from things we've offered.

But generally, those types of responses don't help us improve.

The critical comments, even delivered kindly, are less fun to read. There's a distinct pit in my stomach when I absorb them. It's unpleasant to know that we've somehow missed our goals. I sometimes put such an email aside to read later, when I'm calm and focused, and have a cup of tea and am sitting in my favorite seat, preferably with a blanket and my dog curled up next to me. There may be chocolate involved. Then, I calmly read the comments, breathing evenly, reminding myself that life is good, that this is not an indictment on my whole being, that I am not being threatened, and that this information is precious and valuable—an opportunity to improve my craft. I remember that almost all wisdom comes from experience, from making mistakes, and from learning from them. This moment is that process in action.

No one enjoys critical feedback. But nothing else can improve our game quite like it. And that's why we should ask for it.

Perhaps no one knows this better than Pixar, one of the most successful film studios ever with 14 box office hits in a row. Pixar has a unique model for encouraging critiques within the company to yield the best possible product. As Ed Catmull, president of both Pixar and Walt Disney Animation Studios, said in the Harvard Business Review:

As we built up an animation crew for Toy Story *in the early 1990s, John used what he had learned from Disney and ILM to develop our daily review process. People show work in an incomplete state to the whole animation crew, and although the director makes decisions, everyone is encouraged to comment. There are several benefits. First, once people get over the embarrassment of showing work still in progress, they become more creative. Second, the director or creative leads guiding the review process can communicate important points to the entire crew at the same time. Third, people learn from and inspire each other; a highly creative piece of animation will spark others to raise their game. Finally, there are no surprises at the end: When you're done, you're done. People's overwhelming desire to make sure their work is "good" before they show it to others increases the possibility that their finished version won't be what the director wants. The dailies process avoids such wasted effort.*[8]

As this example shows, soliciting critical feedback along the journey in a safe and supportive environment leads to a much better product.

"Buy yourself a friend"

Now, we're all used to soliciting feedback in work situations. But here's one of my most basic Jewish questions: which is more significant to most people, how they're doing at work or how they're doing at life?

Most people know that what kind of person you are in your relationships with your friends, neighbors, co-workers, and family, is more important than what you achieve professionally. Yet many business concepts that are known to be successful, such as mentorship, peer review, and soliciting constructive criticism, are simply not practiced in our personal lives.

Imagine if we cultivated mentors for life as we did in business. Imagine assembling a team of people (a personal board of directors, as one of my funny friends calls it) each of whom has a unique niche to guide and advise you. Think of a parent, friend, clergy member, wise older person who has lived through more life than you. Maybe some have expertise in work relationships. Others, in parenting. Still others, in spirituality or personal growth. I actually have created such a network for myself and indeed, it's life-changing. Mentorship is important for business. It's even more vital for life.

The ever-relevant text *Ethics of the Fathers* indicates this: "Make for yourself a mentor and buy yourself a friend."[9] The text is specific in its instruction that we need to pro-actively create both vertical relationships (where one is su-perior to the other in wisdom or power) and horizontal relationships (a peer-based connection) in order to be our best selves. What does it mean to "buy" a friend? It doesn't mean you should pay them to be nice to you. It means you should put at least as much research and investment in choosing your friendships as you do in purchasing a new refrigerator. Your friendships are an investment, and they are too vital to who you are just to leave them to chance.

The Ways of the Tzaddikim is another mussar text of anon-ymous authorship. It goes a step further and states that one should always love the person who's willing to tell the truth.[10] So many times we turn to friends because they tell us what we want to hear ("You're right, they're crazy!") rather than gently help us be our best selves.

Imagine if once we had an annual review not only at work, but in our personal lives, with someone we love, respect, and trust. It could be a spouse, a friend, a parent. Now imagine asking this person, "I would like to be the best version of myself. Will you help me? How can I improve? What am I getting right?" Imagine how life-changing this would be! Now imagine doing it monthly, weekly, or even daily, like Pixar! Sounds scary, right? But there is no greater way to improve.

This exercise takes emotional honesty and maturity, and it will challenge our character traits of pride, humility, arrogance, and honesty. We have trouble being objective about ourselves. That's where others come in. If critical feedback is essential for business development, it's far more essential in our personal lives.

"The Torah is acquired in 48 ways… one is to love rebukes."[11] Sometimes critical feedback shows up uninvited and not in a safe, supportive way. Then what?

When my kids were little, they sometimes came home from school complaining about what this one or that one said. "She said I'm stupid! He said I'm mean!" My first question (after validation and empathy, of course) was: Is it true?

This question actually led to a good session of introspection on the part of my little ones. Most of the time, the criticism was untrue. But the child had to critically evaluate the feedback, much as we do as a professional organization, and determine if it needed to be addressed. If it was untrue, we figured out how to deal with the messenger.

But what if it was true? On one memorable occasion someone told my daughter she was mean. I asked my daughter the question: is it true? She thought for a moment and honestly replied, "Sometimes." After giggling in my head, we had a good conversation about what she could do about that.

Can we try this as adults? Next time we receive unpleasant criticism, instead of running to a friend who will staunchly validate us in our self-righteous indignation, what if instead we asked ourselves the simple question, *is it true?*

Sometimes, it is.

Even where criticism is unwanted, unsolicited, and uncalled for, Judaism posits that we should utilize it and metabolize it as a tool for growth. "Who is wise? One who learns from everyone."[12] If we are going to learn from everyone, that includes those whom we wish hadn't spoken.

If the criticism is true, even if the person was out of line, we can still use the information to become better at life. Maybe we even can bring ourselves to a state of gratitude for having come into this valuable information, though it may sting. Can it help us reach a state of improvement? What if it's untrue? How can we utilize the opportunity as a victim to become a stronger and more compassionate person as a result? What conversations could we have with our criticizer to protect ourselves from being hurt?

When we first got a dog four years ago, he used to bark outside until someone let him in. Sometimes we got complaints from a neighbor via text about the barking. My first reaction upon getting these texts was indignation. Of course dogs bark. They are dogs. That's what they do. Isn't part of being a good neighbor overlooking regular neighborhood noises? And shouldn't some things happen with a phone call or a neighborly knock on the door as opposed to an angry text?

The first question I needed to ask myself was whether the complaint was true. Were we being inconsiderate and thoughtless and rude by not preventing our dog from barking outside? I thought about this and decided that the barking was normal and not excessive. But sometimes what one neighbor considers normal noise, another neighbor considers excessive. The criticism, while uninvited and unpleasant, sparked some thoughtful introspection on my part that wouldn't have happened otherwise.

I then had to compose a response that was, in the words of Israel-based educator Rabbi Noach Orlowek, "fair, firm, and friendly."[13] While I don't need to be connected and close with every neighbor, I do want to maintain friendly and polite relationships with them wherever possible. Sometimes this means swallowing criticism that's on my mind, and sometimes it means dealing with criticism that comes my way. I needed to think, write, think, and re-write, but I managed to retain both a neighborly relationship and our dog.

Sometimes criticism comes from strangers. I was on a Facebook group for mothers of special-needs kids. A support group, mind you. I posted a question about how to proceed with a certain issue and was sarcastically criticized by a member of the group. I was astonished at the treatment I got on this "support" group!

So I followed my own advice. I asked myself: *is it true*? Is she right and I'm wrong? And first I reactively decided, NO WAY! Then I sat on it for, oh, about a month. Turned it over in my head. Slept on it. Came back to it. And I decided to take her rude advice.

I couldn't have got to where I am without her. (But I did leave the group. I still need to protect my heart.)

And that's how our worst critics can actually become our greatest coaches—if our goal is not to be comfortable, or complimented, or patted on the back, but to become our best selves via words spoken, whether verbally or digitally.

Obstacles to positive speech

We've already discussed why it's so hard to use our words in a validating way, and why it's tempting to fix others instead. What are some other things that get in the way of using our words constructively?

I think there are two parts to this. First, it can be difficult to remain silent. (We'll look at this challenge in Chapter 6.) Second, it remains tempting to use our words destructively instead of constructively.

The character traits we are building play an important role here. For example, we are often impatient, saying the first tempting thing that comes to mind instead of waiting and considering the outcome of those words. If we haven't exercised and strengthened our self-control muscle, it can be hard to bite back words that ache to be expressed. Arrogance also plays a role, as it does with nearly every trait we explore. Our desire to unload, to be heard, to sound witty or cutting or cute can overpower everything else. And sometimes, it's courage that is missing, when we must clear our throats and say something

The voice of the soul is usually much quieter than the voice of the ego.

difficult, while at the same time saying it in a way that is kind and helpful.

The voice of the soul is usually much quieter than the voice of the ego. By overcoming these obstacles, we make it heard.

Elissa, a 42-year-old mother of two, has been a mussar student for five years. She says:

From the basics of day-to-day living, to my overall happiness and fulfillment, mussar study has transformed my approach to life, to my relationships and the way I view myself. I now look with intention for the humanity and inherent worth we are all born with, and I almost instinctively try to forgive, when in the past, I would have held onto anger or disappointment.

One of the most important relationships in my life is with someone who I deeply love and admire. She is incredibly caring and supportive of me, but she can also be judgmental and confrontational. I have learned it is not my job, and probably not possible, to criticize her and change the difficult aspects of her personality no matter how much I want to.

Instead, I put myself in her shoes, try to understand why she reacts the way she does, and forgive her for the greater good of our relationship, which is absolutely precious to me. Today, there is an overwhelming sense of peace between us and our connection is stronger than ever. I owe that to my mussar study, and specifically, to Ruchi!

CHAPTER 6: SILENCE—A Path to Wisdom

The flip side of the power of speech is the power of silence.

We already know that Jewish mussar texts explore many classically virtuous character traits such as patience, humility, generosity, and honesty. But we also find an unexpected one: silence. *Ethics of the Fathers* teaches, "The vehicle for wisdom is silence."[1] King Solomon tells us, "Closing one's lips makes one thought to be wise."[2] "Thus Rabbi Shimon Ben Gamliel says, 'All my days I grew up among the wise men, and I have found nothing greater [for the body] than silence.'"[3]

To be totally transparent and a tiny bit vulnerable, as I learned these texts and teachings in Jewish day school, I was often left with a vague sense of shame. I am the classic extrovert. I love to talk. I am the first one to volunteer in a group discussion, the first student in class with my hand up. I love cracking jokes in a circle of friends and laughing along with everyone else. All the world's my playground and everyone is a potential friend.

So as I studied the virtues of silence, I realized I had some work to do.

Certainly, my nature is nothing to be ashamed of. Jewish wisdom teaches that God gifted us with the toolbox that is necessary for the spiritual mission we are intended to achieve during our sojourn on this planet.[4] If it's in my toolbox, that's a sign that it is necessary for my mission.

But there's another layer to this idea. Precisely those tools that are NOT "in our toolbox" are those that require our spiritual work. That "missing" tool—for me, silence—may not be our strong suit, and thus not a critical trait for fulfilling our life's work. But one of our jobs in life is the process of self-refinement. Jewish wisdom teaches that we receive our souls in a pure and beautiful state, and at the end of our lives we must return them with interest.[5] During our lives we must polish our inner diamonds and refine the character traits of our souls.

So while I am no longer ashamed of my nature, and I know that God gave me confidence and social strengths for a higher purpose, it is on me to work on cultivating the beautiful trait of silence if I want to become my best self and create my strongest relationships.

How?

Creating space with silence

One of the ways we can cultivate silence is by employing the advantage of time, expressed by the Hebrew phrase *erech apayim,* which literally means '*of long nose'.* The expression is used Biblically to describe God as one who is slow to anger.[6] We've all seen cartoons, and probably emojis, depicting anger by a "steaming" nose. The Biblical phrase reminds us that as we emulate a loving God, we are asked to "lengthen our nose"—to lengthen the distance from stimulus to response.

Anger is a character trait we all possess, though some of us show it more readily and intensely than others. It's hard to control that instinctive feeling of rage that has been externally sparked, but Judaism holds us responsible for what we do with that feeling. The journey from crazy to control can be a long one, and success is measured by the process, not the product. The end goal is to be able to be provoked and... wait. Not to react. To lengthen the space between stimulus and response. Practicing *erech apayim*, then, doesn't look so impressive on the outside, because done well, no one even knows how hard I'm working. It's silent.

We discussed in previous chapters how our behavior patterns can literally change the neural pathways in our brains. So, the more we act a certain way, the more that behavior literally defines us. The more we indulge in rage, the more we strengthen those neural and spiritual pathways that lead to rage. But each time we practice mussar and control ourselves, we also strengthen those neural and spiritual pathways that make us stronger and stronger. As Jewish wisdom says, "Who is strong? One who controls his own drives."[7]

The more we indulge in our rage, the more we strengthen the neural and spiritual pathways to indulge in rage.

A well-known Jewish tale tells about a rabbi who was visited by a married couple in his congregation, complaining about their sad marital story. "Rabbi, we just can't get along! There's so much yelling! You must help us," the wife said. The rabbi listened attentively as each member of the couple described their broken relationship, complete with yelling and angry words. Then he slowly rose and showed them a small vial.

"This is holy water," he pronounced. "It cures anger." The couple looked at him in delight: the answer to their prayers!

"How does it work?" they whispered reverently.

The rabbi instructed them in a grave tone of voice. "Any time you feel angry, take one drop of this holy water and put it on your tongue. Close your mouth and keep it there till your anger dissipates. This miracle water will help you find peace. May your efforts bear fruit." The couple took the water and practically floated home, with great results.

Holy water? Or an ingenious way to keep one's mouth shut in a moment of anger? Or both?

Why is *erech apayim*—simply waiting to respond when provoked —so valuable?

Most of us know when we are saying something mean or damaging. I usually know I'm heading down this wrong road as the words are forming in my brain. We certainly know after the fact, when we feel guilty about the words that we said impulsively. So why don't we stop? Partly, because we have not controlled our anger; our anger has controlled us. In a moment of weakness, of not being in control, we have chosen the easiest response. What we are trying to achieve with the idea of *erach apayim* is creating space so that we can steady ourselves on our feet, reclaim control, re-engage our logical mind, and thus choose more wisely.

Deep inside each one of us is a wise voice—the voice of the soul, also called in Jewish literature the *yetzer hatov*, the positive drive. It's the sound of your conscience, and it knows better. We need to create a space for the wise soulful voice inside us, the voice of our wise self, to drive our responses. This is a spiritual practice that requires discipline and repetition. The first few times you want to try it, you may realize just a bit too late, after you've spoken, that you forgot to wait to react. The next few times, you'll realize during your outburst that you missed your moment of *erech apayim*. But you are growing step by step. And one beautiful day, you'll realize that you have become strong enough to say nothing at all until you've given your wise voice a chance to clear its throat and speak up.

It is often only in the pause, and in the silence, and in the waiting, that our true wisdom can emerge and remind us of better ways to react and to behave.

This process of journeying from reactive to effective is described in a classic mussar text published in 1738 called *The Path of the Just* by Rabbi Moshe Chaim Luzzatto.[8] In it, the author describes nine character traits, each building on the previous trait. The very first is called in Hebrew *zehirut*, commonly translated as "vigilance" or "watchfulness." I prefer the more contemporary words "mindfulness" or "self-awareness."

Here is how Rabbi Luzzatto introduces the trait: "*The idea of mindfulness is for one to be cautious of his deeds and matters, namely, contemplating and watching over his deeds and ways whether they are good or evil; not abandoning his soul to the danger of destruction, God forbid, and not walking through the course of habit like a blind man in darkness. Reason certainly obligates this. For after a person has knowledge and reason to save himself and escape from the destruction of his soul, how is it conceivable that he would willingly blind his eyes from saving himself?"*

In other words, all spiritual character growth must begin with self-awareness—consciousness of who and what one is and isn't. The bad news about self-awareness is that if you don't have it, you don't know that you don't have it. The good news is that just by picking up this book, you are both demonstrating and developing self-awareness. And certainly, by studying it, and deeply considering how its principles apply to you (tempting though it is to think how it actually applies to everyone you know), you are growing your self-awareness deeply, paving the path for all future growth.

Rabbi Luzzatto goes on to build a ladder of growth, moving from mindfulness about negative behaviors on to enthusiasm and energy for positive behaviors, to freedom from blame, to weaning oneself from the pull of materialism, to cleansing oneself of ulterior motives and drives, and on through climbing the mountain until one reaches the pinnacle: holiness. In this book, I have selected the eight character traits I am most passionate about, as I feel they are most sorely lacking in our culture. I also believe these eight traits, when worked on, carry enormous impact for real change in real life in real time. I hope that the traits in this book, too, are a ladder, building one chapter upon another, until we are truly transformed human beings.

This tool—the "lengthening of the nose"—is perhaps one of the most effective ones in relationships. Instead of filling the space with negative, angry and critical words, we can heal a relationship through silence. Expunging those negative moments in parent-child interactions, spousal interactions, issues with neighbors, work-related conflicts, or any other, is the first step to reconnecting with those we love, and staying peaceful with those we don't love.

In our Biblical tradition, we see that our patriarch Jacob calls his children around his deathbed to give them his final blessings. But surprisingly, a number of these "blessings" are actually words of rebuke. Jacob calls out Reuben for his impulsivity and Simeon and Levi for acting on their anger. Rashi, a primary transmitter of ancient wisdom, makes this mind-blowing observation: Jacob noted lots of things over the years that troubled him in his children's behaviors. Yet he said nothing until his deathbed, because he feared he would repel his children from the spiritual path.[10] This connects perfectly with what we discussed in the previous chapter, about ensuring you have the best possible circumstances before offering any rebuke, so that the rebuke may be received and not rejected. This is exactly what Jacob did: close to death, he knew he had his children's full and focused attention.

Talk about creating space between stimulus and response!

"Is what I'm about to say or do…"

It seems that Jacob knew a secret about relationships that many of us forget or haven't assimilated. Before you say something, you must carefully consider the result of your words and their impact on your relationship. Recall the question we discussed earlier based on the work of Dr. William Glasser: *"Is what I'm about to say or do going to bring us closer or further apart?"*

Sometimes, when I come home from an out-of-town work trip, I walk through the doors of my home and here is what I see: the dining room table is piled with homework, snack remains, and mail. The buffet, my husband's domain, is piled with books, bags, bags of books, and random papers. There may or may not be STREAKS on the kitchen counter. I open the fridge and see three started bottles of milk. I go to my car and there are eight half-empty water bottles on the floor and crumpled receipts all over the passenger seat. Also, it smells weird.

Now, I know in my rational mind that my family has done its best to clean up the home before I come home. I know this because we have discussions about things like this. But I can't ignore that all is not up to snuff. My snuff.

What are my options? (After saying hello, of course. And giving hugs and sometimes presents.)

"So guys, just curious, did anyone clean up the house while I was gone? And my car. Who drove my car?" The degree of sarcasm is directly proportional to my fatigue level.

I know this reaction is not helpful. I know it will alienate those who are trying. There is a time and place for these conversations, but not right now. Not right when I get home. Not when they've tried. Not when I'm irritated. Not by hurling rhetorical questions at those I love.

What if we could have a redo?

Let's imagine that before I walk through the door of my home, I spent the ride home mentally preparing myself. The reality is that as awesome as my family is, they don't maintain the home exactly as I do. Part of the price I pay for traveling is a differently maintained home. Let's picture that when I survey the fallout, I think all the same thoughts but don't say them aloud.

What if I just wait, recognize this as a "mussar moment," creating a space (there's *erech apayim*), and saying nothing. Instead I ask myself The Question: *"Is what I'm about to say or do going to bring us closer or further apart?"* And if the answer is "further apart," maybe I can achieve something amazing: saying nothing at all.

The extroversion trap

Silence as a character trait is enjoying somewhat of a renaissance in our culture. As an extrovert who loves to shmooze, I was taken with Susan Cain's landmark book *Quiet: The Power of Introverts in a World That Can't Stop Talking.*[11] She demonstrates that our culture is biased toward extroverts. To be honest, I have benefitted from this bias. I enjoyed popularity in school (and in adulthood) thanks in no small part to my extroversion. Extroverts, defined as those who derive energy from spending time with groups of people, are more likely than their introverted counterparts to speak up in group discussions, work meetings, and college classes. Our society likes this. We think they are smarter, more social, more fun, and more confident.

As Cain writes, "We live with a value system that I call the Extrovert Ideal—the omnipresent belief that the ideal self is gregarious, alpha, and comfortable in the spotlight."[12] (As an interesting aside, Cain's TED Talk begins with her walking onstage with a briefcase filled with books that belonged to her grandfather, who was a rabbi.)

But as *Quiet* methodically indicates, Cain's years of research reveal that while extroverts are more likely to be listened to, introverts are actually more likely to get it right: "If you can think of meetings you've attended, you can probably recall a time—plenty of times—when the opinion of the most dynamic or talkative person prevailed to the detriment of all," she writes.[13] Introverts are more likely to think longer about the issues and process them internally, and only after also hearing what others have to say and turning the idea over for a while in their heads, formulate an opinion that then has the greatest potential to be wise and well thought-out.

From *Quiet*: "It's not that I'm so smart," said Einstein, who was a consummate introvert. "It's that I stay with problems longer."[14]

Jewish wisdom backs up the dangers of being quick to react:

There are seven things that characterize a fool, and seven that characterize a wise man. A wise man does not speak before one who is greater than him in wisdom or age. He does not interrupt his fellow's words. He does not hasten to answer. His questions are on the subject and his answers to the point. He responds to first things first and to latter things later. Concerning what he did not hear, he says "I did not hear." He concedes to the truth. With the fool, the reverse of all these is the case.[15]

This text is bad news for us extroverts. Listen to all the mistakes we make. We overpower others in conversation, answer hastily, do not admit when we do not know. Is it that wise people know to listen first and speak after? Or does the very act of listening increase wisdom? Perhaps both are true.

I have been guilty of sometimes mowing down others in conversation. While my intentions are to be helpful, or to "fix" things (as I admitted earlier), part of my spiritual work is reigning in my desire to speak so others can have a chance. I have learned not to interrupt most of the time—a common pitfall of extroverts. I am learning to cut my monologue short and remembering to ask others about themselves, then practicing good listening skills. Instead of responding to my conversation-mate's words with stories of my own, I can remember to ask her follow-up questions about her own experience, inviting more of her story instead of shifting the conversation back to me. These, for me, have been a learned mussar-infused art. The restraint I describe is a pure act of inner work on my character that ultimately makes me a more spiritually refined human being. The point here is not to squash my natural personality. I believe God created me the way He did for a reason, to serve Him and benefit the world with all the "me-ness" I have. But I do have to channel and temper the natural personality so it's a beautiful garden and not an overgrown bed of weeds. When I do, I feel like a better version of myself, not a smaller one.

It also makes me a better spouse, friend, neighbor, co-work-er and mother. I can't tell you how many professional meet-ings I have sat through where one or two people dominate the conversation and cut others short. Finishing other peo-ple's sentences for them is not cute in a professional setting. It's rude and presumptuous. Trust me—I've made that mis-take more than once.

Refraining from gossip

Jewish law emphasizes restraint in our speech. We can't say everything we want. Words matter. Words can build and words can destroy. It can take a huge effort to muster this kind of restraint, and this effort is considered to be one of the greatest forms of spiritual workout, with the greatest spiritual reward.[16]

Our culture is awash with gossip, but gossip is a pretty big no-no in Judaism. Quite a chunk of our speech-related laws, collectively referred to as *lashon hara* (literally trans-lated, "evil speech") directly speak about gossip, though there are many different kinds of gossip. The parsing out of all the different categories, and the details surrounding how and when things are allowed to be shared, fills many volumes of books and texts in Jewish scholarship.

Let's look at some of the baseline rules, and how they apply to us. The Torah laws about speech teach us not to share negative information about others, whether it's true or untrue. We are warned to be careful about spreading sto-ries—who said what about whom. We are guided about verbal abuse—hurting others directly with our speech—and warned about the seriousness of embarrassing others, especially in public.[17]

There are exceptions to the rules. For example, we are also taught *how* to share negative information about others *when it is necessary and has a constructive purpose*, such as recommending someone for employment or fixing up friends for a blind date. Before sharing this information, we need to confirm not only if the information is true, but if it is also constructive. In other words, could we achieve our goal in any other way without sharing negative information? We should also ask ourselves, could we be exaggerating? Are we certain we are sharing selectively only with those who need to know? Could we perhaps be overly emotional because we have a history with the person? All these need to be explored, and the exploration takes time, honesty, and patience. It can be brutal to keep one's mouth shut when a piece of juicy gossip is just waiting to get out.

In communities we need to be especially mindful about this. Caring about "what the neighbors say" is not smart, but it is a reality that neighbors do chatter. If each individual would resolve not to be that neighbor, imagine what kind of improvements we could see in society.

If you have ever been the topic of someone else's gossip, you know exactly how awful it feels. We often rationalize this kind of chatter, reassuring ourselves that "everyone does it." "It's harmless." "I'm not telling them anything they don't already know." "It will never get back to them." But think how you would feel if you knew others were chattering about you. "Wait, what? They're getting divorced? He gained 40 pounds? They're moving? Their house is in foreclosure? Did you see their daughter? What happened to her? What? He got fired? Why?"

I can't think of a single person who would feel good knowing that kind of gossip is circulating about him. The sage Hillel says: "What is hateful to you, do not do to others."[18] Words matter and therefore silence matters.

In today's Torah community, there are lessons in "guarding our speech," as it's called, via podcasts, daily emails, telephone conferences, and CD sets (remember those?), so they're pretty much available in every form of communication and technology known to humankind, much the same way negative speech is possible on every platform of social communication. The good can always counteract the bad.

That which cannot be heard: giving rebuke

The final type of silence I'd like to focus on builds on what we discussed in the previous chapter about rebuke. Sometimes we should choose *not* to tell someone something, even when we're pretty sure he needs to hear it. And even if we're really, really itching to say it. As Hillel says in *Ethics of the Fathers*, "Do

Words matter and therefore silence matters.

not say something that is not readily understood in the [erroneous] belief that it will ultimately be understood."[19] More pithily, the Talmud spells it out: "Just as there is a mitzvah (obligation) for a person to say something which will be heard, so too there is a mitzvah not to say something which will not be heard."[20]

What does that mean? It means that no matter how important your words are for the other person to hear, don't say them if they're incapable of hearing them.

But if we offer criticism when the person is unable to hear it, we do damage. We alienate the person from us and our values and often spark defensiveness, entrenching them even more strongly in their ways.

Most of us approach words of chastisement like throwing spaghetti at a wall to see what sticks. We generally assume it can't hurt. If they listen, great, and if not, well, it was worth a try.

Judaism and mussar ask us to think deeply before we speak and ask ourselves: what is the purpose of these words? How likely are they to help? If they are useless, or worse, damaging, why say them? Sometimes silence is the biggest mitzvah of the day.

But mostly silence is about ourselves. Can we exercise the restraint we need to not talk? Consider the teaching of Rabbi Nachman of Breslov: "In his youth a person learns how to speak. In his old age, he learns how to keep silent.

Most of us approach words of chastisement like throwing spaghetti at a wall to see what sticks.

What a pity it is that we don't learn how to be silent before we learn how to speak."[21]

Obstacles to silence

Why is it so very hard to remain silent? Which traits lurk beneath this failing of human beings?

When it comes to gossip and criticism, our emotions goad us to say things to relieve our own emotional burden, or to lash out at others with a powerful verbal punch. Controlling our anger and our envy of others is key in controlling our speech to and about them.

To overcome these obstacles, we need to go back to *erech apayim* and learn to breathe through those temptations. We need to remind ourselves that everything happens for a reason, and that if we are triggered, it's a sign that we need to strengthen our character. While silence may feel disempowering, it is actually extremely empowering. We need to remember what we learned earlier: "Who is strong? One who can control his own drives"[22] It's worth it: "Every moment that a person shuts his mouth, he merits the hidden light that no angel or creature can conceive of."[23]

Cindy is a nanny, who married for the first time at the age of 50. She's been studying mussar for two years now:

I always prided myself on telling other people's news, whether it was good or bad. I would be the first one to know, and that was exciting. Knowing people's business made me feel "one up."

Then it got back to people, and they started whispering, "Don't tell Cindy your news. She'll tell others."

It was lashon hara (negative speech), and I never knew that. Then, when I started studying mussar, I learned that it's not nice to share other people's news. It's gossip. I haven't done it since.

Someone reminded me recently about something I said, and I thought, "Today I would never say that." Now I don't want to be friends with people who talk like that. I don't find it attractive. It's not a nice thing to do, and I don't know how to tell them. I want to be the kind of person about whom people say, "She never says anything about anyone." That, to me, is mussar. That is the ultimate compliment.

I used to hurt a lot of people. There was a lot of office gossip. But mussar has made me more aware of my behavior, much more than before, and I'm so proud of myself.

CHAPTER 7: RENEWAL—Coming Home to Yourself

In reading this book thus far, you may have become a bit discouraged by the many ways there are to mess up. To make mistakes. To move further away from our soul's purpose. That can feel like a heavy weight.

But Judaism is big on renewal. The Hebrew word *teshuvah*, commonly translated as repentance, is key here. Literally, *teshuvah* means "return."

Repentance, or renewing oneself, is about returning to who you really are. Judaism leads us through our soul journey on earth. Our souls enable us to fulfill our individual missions. As we travel on this journey, we will make mistakes and make smudge marks on the beautiful soul we have been gifted with. But we have the power to "return," to bring the soul back to its perfection.

The steps we have explored in this book can help us get there. Through working on ourselves and developing our traits of giving favorable judgment, forgiveness, acceptance of others, generosity, and using our speech for positive purposes, our pathway to renewal is made smoother. We have learned to recognize where we are most likely to mess up, and to strengthen ourselves and our "better angels" in our ability to choose the right path, both in speech and in action. This is how we pave the road to *teshuva*.

Rabbi Abraham Isaac Kook was one of the fathers of religious Zionism, Chief Rabbi of British Mandatory Palestine in the Land of Israel in the early 1900's, and a renowned sage and thinker. He taught:

A person's life is perfected by developing his inherent character. And since one's still-undeveloped character lacks insight, sin is guaranteed along this path of development. "There is no righteous person in the land who will commit good and not sin." [Ecclesiastes 7:20]....Therefore, teshuvah repairs the damage [caused by sin and trying to be someone you are not] and restores the world and this person's life to its root, precisely by helping the inherent character to develop.[1]

The power of renewal

The Torah teaches that repentance is the ultimate renewal, literally changing who we are. Not only that, but a person who has erred and repaired is at a higher level of spiritual refinement and is even more evolved than one who has not fallen at all. Ancient Jewish wisdom teaches, "In the place that a *ba'al teshuvah* (someone who has conquered his or her flaws) stands, a purely righteous person is not worthy to stand."[2]

Do you remember back in Chapter 1, when I explained how God gave the Jewish people the gift of forgiveness, through the Day of Atonement, Yom Kippur? The Jews had miscalculated the time when Moses should have descended from Mount Sinai, and in their panic, they created an idol, the Golden Calf. God's ability to forgive His people led to the next gift, the holiday of Sukkot. The holiday is in the fall, after the High Holidays, and commemorates the protective shelters that God gave the Israelites in the desert. We build outdoor huts with thatched roofs where we take our meals and sometimes even sleep, for the duration of the holiday. We replicate these God-given shelters that protected us from the elements as well as from enemies, and re-experience the faith of living only with God's protection alone.

The weird thing is that the Israelites had been granted those shelters six months prior, after the Exodus in the spring! In fact, they lost the special protection after sinning with the Golden Calf! We are, it seems, commemorating the *return* of the booths after the Israelites were forgiven. Odd.

Rabbi Elijah ben Solomon Zalman, an 18th-century Lithuanian Talmudist, kabbalist, and Jewish leader also known as the Vilna Gaon (sage of Vilna), sheds light on how this episode illuminates the power of renewal.[3] The true beauty of a relationship is not in the honeymoon phase, before we've shown our humanity in all its flawed glory. The true litmus test of any relationship is what happens after the fall, after the fight.

He explains that after Yom Kippur, after God forgave us, He re-gifted us with the clouds of protective glory. The making up, the renewal, brings even more closeness and preciousness than we had in the initial stages of the relationship. It is the reconnection of our relationship with God that explains why Sukkot is called the "season of our joy."

As we also explored earlier, the relationships that matter most to us, such as with spouses, close friends, siblings, parents and children, all experience conflict. But, like the Jews and God back in the desert more than 3,000 years ago, when we make up after having had real, difficult, and honest conversations, we often find ourselves closer than ever before.

If God loves us so much when we've renewed ourselves, can we love ourselves at least as much?

Our mistakes, missteps, and messes are never the problem. God created humans, not robots and not angels. The problem is when we get stuck and choose to do nothing about it. However, when our errors and misjudgments become an opportunity to renew ourselves, the stumbling blocks transform into building blocks.

King Solomon declares, "The righteous one falls seven times, yet gets back up."[4] On the surface, this verse seems to indicate that righteous people have resilience. They stumble in their spiritual journeys, but they keep rising and trying again. In a letter to one of his students, Rabbi Yitzchok Hutner of blessed memory, who was my grandfather's rabbi and dean of the Chaim Berlin Rabbinical Seminary, suggests something deeper. Precisely because this person fell seven times, each time he was able to rise to higher heights. Each time he regressed, he learned something new about himself and became a wiser, better human being. Each stay in spiritual rehab taught him deeper truths about staying clean. It is the falling, and only the falling, that affords him the opportunity to become righteous.

Regret, guilt, and shame—what good are they?

One of the most important ingredients of *teshuvah,* of repentance, is regretting one's actions.[5] True regret is an emotion that leads to action. It is important to distinguish among regret, guilt, and shame. These are all powerful emotions, but only one is a catalyst for growth. The other two keep us imprisoned and unable to progress. Which is which?

If you cringe when you look back at the things you used to do, say, or believe, if you are embarrassed at the person you used to be, that discomfort is called "regret." It's positive. It means you are a growing human being. Get comfortable with that discomfort because you can't grow without it. The key is not to wallow in this emotion, but to use it as a springboard for new heights of personal and spiritual growth.

Actress Tracee Ellis Ross said it well when she said, "I am learning every day to allow the space between where I am and where I want to be to inspire me and not terrify me."[6]

Guilt is a different thing altogether. The difference between regret and guilt is that regret compels you to examine and change your behaviors, while guilt traps you in a negative loop. For some reason, guilt is considered very Jewish, but I loudly protest. Guilt is not Jewish! Judaism is about growing, not staying stuck and making excuses. Sometimes I wonder if people feel guilty when they don't know how to change or grow. Perhaps they think, *I'm feeling guilty, so at least I'm doing something about it: feeling guilty!*

Unfortunately, guilt is debilitating. Sometimes people feel guilty when other people are being really nice to them. *I feel so guilty that you went out of your way.* To this I say: Don't feel guilty, feel grateful! Turn the guilt around to the flip side, gratitude, and say, *Thank you so much for going out of your way.*

If we feel guilty because of our previous actions, we can instead try to elevate guilt to regret. We can do this by asking, *What can I learn from this? How am I a different person because of this?* Don't feel guilty—fix it!

There is another category of guilt worth exploring for a moment. If we feel guilty because of behaviors we engaged in *before* we knew they were wrong or understood that they were against our best interests, we can forgive ourselves. Tell yourself: *I did the best I could with the tools I had. Now that I know better, I do better.* Release the guilt and find peace.

As we've established, Judaism is about action. Feelings that compel positive behavior are great. Feelings that keep us stuck are negative.

Spiritually, true regret means, *I am simply not that person anymore.* If I could go back in time and revise history, I would. It also means that if there is anything I can repair right now, I will. I'll apologize sincerely (remember our chapter on forgiveness) and make restitution wherever possible. God promises that if we engage in this process sincerely, He will indeed erase history. Those mistakes will be completely stricken from our record.

Feelings that compel positive behavior are great. Feelings that keep us stuck are negative.

Where does shame come in? Is it appropriate, in the process of renewal, to feel shame for our actions? Is that a helpful or useful emotion?

135

According to Brené Brown, a researcher at the University of Houston and author of the bestselling book *The Gift of Imperfection*, shame is an "intensely painful feeling or experience of believing that we are flawed and therefore unworthy of love and belonging."[7] It's an emotion that affects all of us and profoundly shapes the way we interact in the world.

Using this as our working definition, shame has absolutely no place in our psyche, because we are all children of God. Yes, we are all flawed, but we are all worthy of love and belonging despite being flawed. Our imperfections make us human. They provide the testing ground for us to evolve.

God certainly agrees, as we'll see from this astonishing ancient Jewish teaching about the giving of the Torah at Sinai:

Rabbi Yehoshua ben Levi said: When Moses ascended on High to receive the Torah, the ministering angels said before the Holy One, Blessed be He, "Master of the Universe, what is this mortal human doing here among us?" The Holy One, Blessed be He, said to them: "He came to receive the Torah." The angels said before Him: "The Torah is a hidden treasure that was concealed by you for generations before the creation of the world, and you seek to give it to flesh and blood? ...The rightful place of God's majesty, the Torah, is in the heavens."

The Holy One, Blessed be He, said to Moses: "Provide them with an answer as to why the Torah should be given to the people." ...Moses said before Him: "Master of the Universe, the Torah that You are giving me, what is written in it?" God said to him: "I am the Lord your God Who brought you out of Egypt from the house of bondage" (Exodus 20:2). Moses said to the angels: "Did you descend to Egypt? Were you enslaved to Pharaoh? Why should the Torah be yours?"

Again Moses asked: "What else is written in it?" God said to him: "You shall have no other gods before Me" (Exodus 20:3). Moses said to the angels: "Do you dwell among the nations who worship idols that you require this special warning?"

Again Moses asked: "What else is written in it?" The Holy One, Blessed be He, said to him: "Remember the Shabbat day to sanctify it" (Exodus 20:8). Moses asked the angels: "Do you perform labor that you require rest from it?"

Again Moses asked: "What else is written in it?" "Do not take the name of the Lord your God in vain" (Exodus 20:7), meaning that it is prohibited to swear falsely. Moses asked the angels: "Do you conduct business with one another that may lead you to swear falsely?"

Again Moses asked: "What else is written in it?" The Holy One, Blessed be He, said to him: "Honor your father and your mother" (Exodus 20:12). Moses asked the angels: "Do you have a father or a mother that would render the commandment to honor them relevant to you?"

Again Moses asked: "What else is written in it?" God said to him: "You shall not murder, you shall not commit adultery, you shall not steal" (Exodus 20:13). Moses asked the angels: "Is there jealousy among you, or is there an evil inclination within you that would render these commandments relevant?" Immediately they agreed with the Holy One, Blessed be He, that He made the right decision to give the Torah to the people... [8]

In this astounding narrative, the angels protest the giving of God's word to humans because humans are flawed. Moses stunningly uses those very flaws to prove why they need the Torah more than any perfect angel.

The angels knew exactly what was in the Torah. But they didn't understand why God would risk allowing the Torah to descend to our lowly, materialistic world, filled with self-ishness and base desires. They were saying, we, the angels, will appreciate and cherish the Torah and humans will not.

Moses responded that the very purpose of the Torah is to civilize humanity, and therefore it *must* descend to our low-ly and physical world. This is exactly where God wants to be, because this is the only arena where humans can transform with the power of renewal, from darkness to light. This is, in fact, precisely the purpose of the universe. There is absolutely no shame in being profoundly flawed and human.

There is absolutely no shame in being pro-foundly flawed and human.

Our struggle to keep rising after we fall is what gives meaning to our journeys, our choices, and our lives. Living life "safely" is not only meaningless, it's completely unrealistic. Thomas Edison famously said, "I have not failed 10,000 times. I have not failed once. I have succeeded in proving that those 10,000 ways will not work."

Failure and human imperfection are not shameful. They are the starting points for growth.

In light of the above, I'd define our terms as such:

Regret: The feeling that I did something bad, from which I will now move on.

Guilt: The feeling that I did something bad and can't move on from it.

Shame: The feeling that I did something bad and that means I am bad.

Obstacles to renewal

What prevents us from renewing ourselves?

The classic mussar text *The Path of the Just* teaches that one of the biggest obstacles to growth is our constant "busy-ness"—and it was written in the 1700's![9] Imagine what the author would say to our modern 24/7 digital enslavement. We're always so busy, busy, busy doing all kinds of important and urgent things so that we don't have time to introspect and reflect on the spiritual and moral quality of our lives. Journalist Laura Vanderkam writes:

Instead of saying "I don't have time" try saying "it's not a priority," and see how that feels. Often, that's a perfectly adequate explanation. I have time to iron my sheets, I just don't want to. But other things are harder. Try it: "I'm not going to edit your résumé, sweetie, because it's not a priority." "I don't go to the doctor because my health is not a priority." If these phrases don't sit well, that's the point. Changing our language reminds us that time is a choice. If we don't like how we're spending an hour, we can choose differently.[10]

Author Stephen Covey popularized this story about time management:

A teacher comes into class and shows the kids a gallon-sized glass jar. He brings out a bowl of large rocks and dumps them into the jar until they reach the top.

He asks the class if the jar is full, to which they naturally reply, yes.

Then, the professor brings out a bowl of pebbles, and proceeds to pour them into the jar. He shakes the jar until the pebbles settle in all the spaces between the big rocks. He asks again if the jar is now full. The class responds yes.

Lastly, the professor reveals a bucket of sand, which he pours into the jar until every nook and cranny is occupied. The jar finally appears full—until the professor pours a bottle of water into the jar.

"Now it's full," he says. "What is the moral of the story?"

The kids come up with various theories, such as, "There's always room for more." But then the teacher reveals the meaning: "If we had put the sand in first, would there have been any room for the big rocks?"[11]

I teach this story to my groups, explaining that the large rocks represent our biggest priorities in life. I challenge my students to come up with the three or four biggest "rocks" of their lives. Most will say family, faith, community, health, friends, self-care. But many will confess that they don't actually put those rocks in their calendars first. We often focus on what is urgent rather than on what is important. The time-sensitive, "urgent" demands often steal our precious minutes and attention away from the less demanding "important" issues and priorities of our lives. President Eisenhower said, "I have two kinds of problems: the urgent and the important. The urgent are not important, and the important are never urgent."

Judaism provides an antidote to the constant "busy-ness" through Shabbat, the Sabbath. Recall the conversation between the angels and Moses—humans need Shabbat because we work so much. We desperately need that respite from the dinging and pinging, from the frenetic demands on our time and attention. What are we supposed to do on Shabbat? Focus on all the things that my students cite as the "rocks" of their lives: family, faith, community, friends, health, and self-care.

Take a breather from work. Power down your devices. Share festive meals with friends and family. Join as communities to worship and pray. Take walks. Read books. Nap. Play games. Have meaningful conversations and use the distance from the mundane, workaday world to get perspective.

The quality and direction of our actions and our priorities is our most important focus in this world. Let's make time for it.

There are other obstacles to renewal.

In addition to our frenetic activity, I think many of us don't really believe that our actions actually matter. This is where faith comes in. Judaism teaches that God is a loving being who deeply cares about each and every one of us. Our lives matter, our thoughts matter, and God notices every single thing that we do. Each one of us was created completely unique and customized: a limited-edition, artisanal work of art. And in fact, the Torah teaches us that no human being will suffer for even a moment longer than necessary.

If we each remember how deeply important we are to God, how much we matter and the impact of our intentions, motivations, and efforts, we'd be far more prepared to do something significant to change our lives for the better. We've discussed in previous chapters the powerful effect of a small shift in words of validation and the value of taking even small steps toward forgiveness. Small actions can have a profound ripple effect.

Still, change is hard, and we tend to be lazy because we know it is hard. It's also annoying. None of us likes to face our flaws—how much more tempting to distract ourselves with Netflix, alcohol, or sleep. Our culture wants to "fix" or medicate our angst, but we know that fixing is an inside job. No one can fix you but you. No pill, no mantra, no therapist. It will always come right down to you doing the work of facing your flaws, of learning new and uncomfortable habits, of twisting and stretching yourself into your best you.

We often lose hope in ourselves. Perhaps we've tried to change before and fallen. We've failed and failed again. It's so hard to keep trying, and this despair is yet another obstacle to renewal. But in the words of the Israeli national anthem, "*Od lo avdah tikvateinu,*" we have not lost our hope, "*hatikvah bat shnot alpayim,*" the hope that is 2,000 years old. As a Jewish nation, we still stand two millenia after the destruction of our Temple by the Romans and our exile from Israel. We still hope and pray, every single day, for the rebuilding of our Temple in Jerusalem and for an era of national unity and world peace. This abiding faith and hope referring to a national dream should be a beacon to each of us in our personal lives as well.

Judaism is patient. God is patient. We must be patient with ourselves. True growth is never fast and never easy. Don't despair—it's the journey that matters, because the destination is, and has always been up to God.

On the other hand, some people have the opposite problem. They're overconfident and blind to their flaws. As we've mentioned, arrogance can be an obstacle to developing many good character traits, and renewal is no exception. Harboring an overinflated sense of our own moral superiority is a very dangerous barrier to self-awareness, and without self-awareness, there is no growth.

Finally, I think it's tempting to look around at what "everyone else is doing" and use that as a moral barometer for ourselves. In the story of Noah and the flood, Noah is called a "righteous man in his generation." The rabbis of the Talmud differ on the implication of this phrase.[12] Perhaps Noah was especially righteous in the context of how corrupt his generation was and how hard he had to work to resist becoming influenced by them. Others interpret it to mean that Noah's righteousness was only in comparison to his neighbors. In another generation, he might have been just mediocre. Given the competition, he looked pretty good.

Actually, both realities can be true. When "everyone else" is behaving badly, it's more of an achievement to rise above the cultural trends. But you can't *True growth is never fast and never easy.* use shoddy communal norms as a baseline for where your work is. If you want to live your best life, you can only compare yourself to you. Who was I yesterday? Whom do I want to be tomorrow? Those are the only questions that matter. Everyone else is either an inspiration or a distraction.

Giselle, who's been studying mussar with me online after I led her group's Israel trip, is a 40-year-old wife and stay-at-home mom with two kids under the age of 10. She says:

Every day of my life from the moment I wake up to the moment I go to bed I try my best to think how I can improve in my home and with my friends and community. I try to be more patient with my kids and husband especially! I try to be patient with my parents and father and mother-in-law. Oh… this is definitely an area that I need to be mindful of. My mother-in-law has dementia and she forgets a lot, and this has taught me to be mindful that she needs to be reassured she is loved instead of me being impatient with her. I try not to get upset.

I have definitely changed in my laziness, I think about what I am about to do before taking action. I wake up and as soon as I wake up I try to pray before I forget and I always thank God for giving me health and a beautiful family.

I try to stay calm throughout my day, and act with deliberation. This one is especially hard when I am tired! But I try to be mindful before bursting into anger. But above all I always think that I should do all this because I am so blessed and I should try to give the best of myself to others.

Thank you Ruchi for your amazing teachings! The world needs more mussar. Thank you! Thank you! For now, I may go back and listen to all of your teachings again, since I feel very worried and your teachings calm my nerves.

CHAPTER 8: HAPPINESS—Another Inside Job

We have arrived at our final character trait: happiness. Aren't we happier already? It would seem that after working on forgiveness, on letting go of judgment, on acceptance of others and generosity toward them, on harnessing the power of speech and silence, and on the transformative potential of renewal, that this would be the natural result. Perhaps we view happiness as the destination of it all. Haven't we Americans been promised in the Declaration of Independence that it is, "self-evident that all men… are endowed by their Creator with certain unalienable rights, that among these are life, liberty and the pursuit of happiness"?

Even though God loves us very much, Judaism does not view the pursuit of happiness as an inalienable right. But maybe we first need to understand how Judaism defines happiness. What is it really? How do we get it?

Happiness is a choice

In Chapter 4 we discussed love, which, like happiness, is an emotion that people are constantly pursuing. Every artist and poet has a take on the elusive attainment of happiness. Just as we established that love is a choice and a behavior, even an obligation, perhaps happiness is the same.

Just as the Torah commands us to love our neighbor and to love God, implying that love is a choice, listen to what it tells us about happiness: "And you shall be happy with all the good that God has given you and your household."[1]

It seems that God is asking us to take control of our own happiness, to put the keys to happiness in our own pockets. Happiness is neither a destination nor an award bestowed by forces outside of ourselves. Happiness, like love, is a behavior, a choice, a direct result of our own actions. Happiness is a character trait that we need to work on.

Happiness, like love, is a behavior, a choice, a direct result of our own actions.

Let's see how the Torah helps us to understand this.

The verse above follows the section of first fruits. When a farmer in the land of Israel harvests his first fruits, he needs to bring them to Jerusalem as a gift to the Temple. This is the commandment known as *bikkurim*. He recites a declaration chronicling many key points in Jewish history, including the journey of our nation from the perfidy of Laban, Jacob's deceitful father-in-law, through the terrible persecution of our people in Egypt, describing the miraculous Exodus and, finally, our arrival in the Land of Israel, a "land flowing with milk and honey." On this triumphant note of gratitude, we are to place the basket of fruits before God, and… be happy.[2]

Unpacking this in context leads us to several important insights about how to go about strengthening the character trait of happiness in the modern era.

First, it teaches us that happiness is inextricably linked with gratitude. Gratitude is the precursor to joy. More on that soon. Second, notice the verbal declaration of gratitude. The Torah is teaching us that we must articulate our national and personal journeys, noting where God has brought about positive change in our lives and answered our prayers. Each one of us has an amazing trajectory. Incredible things that have happened to us, people we've met who have changed our lives, tremendous opportunities that seemed to fall in our laps "accidentally". How often do we take the opportunity to look back and trace these journeys, reclaiming our relationship with God and His role in our lives? Doing this is the path to happiness.

Gratitude is the precursor to joy.

We think happiness is outside of us, a destination where we have yet to arrive. *When I meet someone special, I'll be happy. When my career is on track, I'll be happy. When my father finally acknowledges my success, I'll be happy. When the kids make something of themselves, I'll be happy.* But happiness is an inside job. Happiness is about paying attention to everything we already have. Happiness is the choice to notice God's love and care in gifting us with all the beautiful things in our past and present. Happiness is choosing joy in our current lives, exactly as they are.

Rabbi Eliyahu Eliezer Dessler, a mussar master, Talmud scholar, and philosopher of the 20th century, teaches that we often think that wealth will bring us happiness, yet we see that wealthy people are at risk of being unhappy, spoiled, bored and jealous.[3] Wealth isn't the problem, though. Poor people are often anxious and depressed. The middle class gets squeezed on both sides. It seems that money is a challenge no matter how much you have, or don't have. Although everyone might want to win the lottery, money and happiness are complicated bedfellows.

The book *The Path of the Just* teaches us the very purpose for which the world was created. Why did God create the universe? Things were fine before humans came along. The only thing an all-powerful God was "lacking," so to speak, was a beneficiary for His kindness. So God created this world for us, His creations, His children. The world was created for giving, to give us joy.[4]

We mentioned in Chapter 3, when discussing accepting others, that one purpose of our journey on this planet is to become more holy, more Godly people, and to cultivate those traits in others. We are here to improve and refine ourselves, and also, we are here to make a positive impact on others and on the world. The truth is that both these aspects have the power to increase our joy. Living a life of meaning by working on ourselves fills us with joy and purpose. Making the world a better place also fills us with meaning and purpose, and reminds us that we are deeply important and necessary to the fabric of the universe. In this way, God's creation of humankind for the purpose of blessing us with his kindness is partnered with our efforts down here in which we earn that kindness and blessing by dint of our own efforts to be better and do better. Earned pleasure, the hard-earned glow of a job well done, is often its own reward.

Yet we often remove ourselves from that joy. *Ethics of the Fathers* teaches, "Envy, desire, and glory remove a person from this world."[5] While the world was created to give us joy, many of us remove ourselves from that joy by capitulating to the traits of envy, desire, and glory. Our materialistic world honors celebrity status, the precise sort of status we have learned will have the opposite effect on our happiness. When we feel bad about what others have and we do not, we have fallen into the envy trap. Every advertisement we see urges our materialistic desires for more and more physical possessions. And glory is the hankering for honor, attention, and esteem.

I once heard the following spot-on equation: happiness = reality ÷ expectations. The more we hope to acquire, whether by envying others, desiring stuff, or coveting honor, the smaller our chance that reality will deliver on those yearnings and the greater the opportunity for dissatisfaction. But, if we lower expectations and actively remove ourselves from envy, desire, and honor, we raise our happiness sum. The more money we have, the greater our needs grow—unless we consciously choose to live beneath our means, noticing all the good we already have, and asking ourselves, "Do we really need that?"

Judaism wants us to be happy. In fact, Judaism is so into happiness that that there are at least 14 words in the Torah to describe joy.[6] They're all different (kind of like saying "inclement weather" in Cleveland).

Here they are:

Simchah is the broadest word for joy, and indicates total happiness in its fullest. It's also used to describe a joyous occasion, such as a wedding or birth of a baby.

Chedvah is pure, unfiltered joy and indicates the joy of being with others.

Ditzah is awe-inspiring joy that makes you want to dance.

Gilah is a strong sensation that bursts forth but can dissipate quickly.

Hana'ah means to enjoy something specific, such as a fine meal or beautiful sunset.

Nachas is the satisfying contentment arising from joy, especially from our children or something we have created.

Osher is a deep sense of joy, feeling blessed in a way that satisfies our yearning for inner peace and meaning.

Orah means "light" and "joy," where education and awareness inspires and lifts us.

Pitzchah is joy that makes us burst into song.

Ra'anan is when we're so overcome with joy that we cry or shout happily.

Rinah is joy that shows itself in song.

Sasson is a happiness that comes unexpectedly.

Teruah is joy in a shout or cheer. This word is used for the sound a shofar makes.

Tzahalah combines happiness with dancing.

How amazing is it that we can look at all these variations of happiness, all the things that can prompt it and all the ways we can express it? I think this teaches us that much more happiness can be ours, if we choose it. All of these flavors of happiness are in our hands.

The gratitude connection

Let's get back to the story of the first fruits, the *bikkurim*. The ceremony and blessing are built around expressions of gratitude. What's the relationship between happiness and gratitude?

We've already established that raising our awareness of how much we already have expands our "reality" dividend in our happiness equation. The more we perceive that we have, the greater our happiness quotient. So in addition to working on lowering our expectations by divesting ourselves of envy, desire, and honor, let's now focus on raising our perception of how blessed we are, broadening our reality factor to achieve greater degrees of joy.

Judaism is literally named for gratitude. Our matriarch Leah's fourth son Judah, "Yehuda" in Hebrew, was given his name based on the Hebrew word for gratitude. After giving birth, Leah said, "This time I shall give thanks to God," and the verse continues to tell us that for this reason she named him Judah.[7] Rashi, a prominent transmitter of ancient wisdom, comments that each of Jacob's four wives knew that there were to be 12 tribes. The assumption was that each would bear three sons. When Leah bore a fourth, it *exceeded her expectations*. Now she really felt blessed—she got more than she'd expected. Jews are known as *yehudim*, grateful ones, as we must carry that trait within our very identity. (The 'y' sound in Hebrew often becomes a 'j' in English.) We see that lowering our expectations is tied to realizing how very blessed we are. They go hand-in-hand.

Jewish law teaches us that each morning we are to wake up with the following words on our lips, spoken even before we get out of bed (even before we check Facebook): "*Modeh ani lefanecha, melech chai v'kayam, she-hechezarta bi nishmati b'chemlah, rabbah emunatecha.* I am grateful before You, living and eternal King, that you have restored my soul to me with compassion. How great is Your faith in me!"[8]

This small prayer is a crash course in gratitude. Give thanks first thing in the morning. Say it aloud, don't just think it. Tell God you are grateful to Him. Specify what you are grateful for: life, faith, compassion. Acknowledge that God has faith in you, even if you don't have faith in yourself. He has granted you another day! This means you can achieve something important. Finally, recognize how amazing your life is!

I like to follow up my "*Modeh ani* practice" with a customized, specific thing that I am grateful for that day. "Today, God, I am grateful for the sunshine. Today, God, I am grateful for my beautiful bedroom. Today, God, I am grateful for my daughter. Today, God, I am grateful that I have a job."

It is literally impossible to start your day with this type of verbal, specific gratitude and not feel happier.

Happiness is already in your soul

In its chapter on the character trait of joy, the mussar text *Ways of the Righteous* teaches that happiness comes from accepting that everything God gives you is for the best. It lists four ingredients in the journey to joy, emphasizing acceptance at each stage:

1. Showing trust in God in the way we act.
2. Having faith in God in our minds and attitudes.
3. Using our intelligence and logic to remind ourselves that everything happens for a reason.
4. Being content with what we have.[9]

By way of illustration, King David, who lived a very difficult life, wrote 150 psalms expressing every form of human emotion as a prayer to God. Here is Psalm 131:

A song of ascents to David. God, my heart did not become arrogant and my eyes didn't become uplifted, and I did not pursue things that were too great or wondrous for me. I swear that I calmed and quieted my soul, like a nursing baby on its mother, my soul was like a nursing baby with me. May Israel hope toward God from now until forever.

In this short psalm, King David expresses the secret to contentment. Don't look outside of yourself for things that are greater than yourself. Don't compare your reality to someone else's highlight reel. Have more modest expectations. Turn to God to sustain you—there's the faith we talked about from *The Ways of the Righteous*. Let that faith calm and quiet your soul. Everything that happens to us is destined for a reason. No one can take away what God intended to be for you. No one can diminish your light or steal your thunder unless it is determined by God. Let this infuse you to be content with all the ways that God already sustains you.

Happiness is not outside of you. It is within you. It is already in your soul. Turn to God and find it.

There is a Talmudic teaching, *gam zu l'tovah*—everything happens for the best. This is not an easy belief for many people because life has so many hard things in it. Like all eight traits that we are exploring, it takes dedicated, patient effort to get to the point where we can make this belief our own. One of the most beautiful examples of this attitude was demonstrated dramatically by Rabbi Akiva, one of the most famous Jewish sages of ancient times.

Rabbi Akiva was walking along the road and came to a certain city. He inquired about lodging and they did not give him any. He said: Everything that God does, He does for the best. He went and slept in a field, and he had with him a rooster, a donkey and a candle. A gust of wind came and extinguished the candle; a cat came and ate the rooster; and a lion came and ate the donkey. He said: Everything that God does, He does for the best. That night, an army came and took the city into captivity. It turned out that Rabbi Akiva alone, who was not in the city and had no lit candle, noisy rooster or donkey to give away his location, was saved. He said to them: Didn't I tell you? Everything that God does, He does for the best.[10]

Aside from the incredible clarity that Rabbi Akiva possessed in seeing exactly how his apparent stresses were actually for the best, notice his serenity and sense of calm along the journey. We might not always see in the moment, or even in this lifetime, how our difficulties are for our good, but the sense of peace and joy that comes from accepting God's will is irreplaceable. How many times do we stress out, only to realize later that we worried for nothing? Or worse, worried about all the wrong things?

Adopting an attitude of faith gives us permission to choose joy in the moment even when things are going all wrong. Counting our blessings and excelling at gratitude helps us feel joyful and boosts our ability to make faith real.

In my home I have a ceramic bowl that a dear friend gave me for my birthday. It says in Yiddish and English: "*Az mir ken nisht haben vos mir vill, darf men villen vos mir habt. If you can't have what you want, then want what you have.*"

Two Jewish holidays, Chanukah and Purim, are celebrated with much pomp and ceremony. Both were established to joyously acknowledge God's miracles. And yet, both holidays commemorate miracles in history that left us in a compromised political and spiritual state. For example, the story of Purim took place in the 4th century BCE. The Jews had been exiled by the Babylonians after the destruction of the first Temple, and were living in Persia. The evil Haman had bribed the king in order to get permission to kill every Jew in the empire. He failed. But after the Jews were saved, they remained living under foreign rule. They did not immediately

Adopting an attitude of faith gives us permission to choose joy in the moment even when things are going all wrong.

get permission to return to Israel or to rebuild their Temple. Queen Esther, the Jewish heroine of the story, remained married to King Ahasuerus, an amoral man, living a solitary life outside the Jewish community until her dying day.

The Chanukah story, which took place around the second century BCE, describes the oppressive rule of the Syrian-Greeks over Israel, the Jewish military victory over these enemies, and the miracle of the oil and rededication of the Temple. But once again, looking at the larger historical context, the Jews were far from okay. Their leadership was compromised, the Syrian-Greeks were still calling the shots, and the second Temple was destroyed about a century later.

In the bigger scheme of history, how significant were the miracles? Wasn't the joy short-lived?

Perhaps this, then, is the miracle: Although our troubles didn't magically disappear, we, as a nation, were privileged to feel God supporting us through those troubles.[11] This alone is enough to warrant joy. If we want to strengthen our character trait of joy, we need to remember, in the timeless words of Bette Midler, "God is watching us from a distance." Life may be tough, but God is on your team.

Laughter and faith

Judaism doesn't only believe in joy and happiness. It believes in the power of laughter, too. Laughter often arises during the unexpected, perhaps when we see the least expected outcome or statement. We laugh when we see that things can suddenly change for the better (or when the unexpected takes us by surprise). As contemporary scholar, physician, and philosopher Rabbi Akiva Tatz teaches, "[there is a] mystical concept that the response to deliverance from imminent disaster is the root of laughter." [11]

Our matriarch Sarah was the first to laugh in the Torah. She laughed when God told her she was going to give birth to a baby in her old age.[12] In fact, her baby's name, Isaac, "Yitzhak," means "he will laugh." His birth had seemed so improbable!

Rabbi Akiva was known not only for his ability to see everything from God as for the good as we saw above, but was also known for laughing when everyone else was crying:

Four sages, Rabban Gamaliel, Rabbi Elazar ben Azariah, Rabbi Joshua, and Rabbi Akiva, were traveling together.

They came to Jerusalem, the once-teeming city, now laid utterly to waste. When they came to Mount Scopus, overlooking the city, they tore their clothes in grief. When they reached the Temple Mount, they saw a fox, running from the spot where the Holy of Holies had once stood. They all burst into tears, except for Rabbi Akiva, who laughed. The other sages said to him: "How can you laugh at this scene of such destruction?" He said to them: "Why do you weep?" They replied: "We weep, for the place which was once the Holy of Holies, which no outsider could enter, now is desolate, inhabited by wild beasts. How could we not weep?"

Akiva said, "And that is why I laugh. I saw enacted before my eyes the terrible words of the prophet Uriah, 'Zion is plowed over like a desolate field.' That gave me the faith to hope that I would see the fulfillment of the comforting words of the prophet Zechariah, 'Once again the aged will rest in the broad avenues of Jerusalem.' If our worst fears can come true, so too can our greatest hopes." They said to him, "Akiva, you have comforted us." [13]

Notice how all our themes about happiness come together in this narrative: lowering of expectations, faith that everything God does is for the best, acceptance of what is, and hope for a better tomorrow.

Obstacles to happiness

We all want to be happy, so let's look at what keeps us from feeling that wonderful emotion. Some are internally driven, and some externally driven.

The advertising industry is designed to mess with our psychology and make us unhappy. If we're unhappy, maybe buying this new piece of jewelry or going for a facial will do the trick. Advertising creates a problem that its product can ostensibly fix. It sounds simplistic and easy to see through, but the messages are insidious. They infiltrate our brains. They disrupt our serenity. This is good for the economy, but bad for happiness.

Notice how many campaigns shamelessly co-opt the language of joy to convince you that happiness is just one product away:

Trident: *A little piece of happy.* McDonald's: *Wake up happy.* Coca-Cola: *Open happiness.* Pepsi: *Happiness is a choice* (the choices pictured are Pepsi, Pepsi Max, and Diet Pepsi). *Happiness is a cigar called Hamlet.*

Pay close attention to the often-transparent message that products will make you happy. My husband and I went on vacation once to Atlanta, Georgia. We visited the iconic Coca-Cola museum there and, like good tourists, settled in to watch the 8-minute film.

The movie was complete and shameless Coca-Cola advertising, pure and simple. It featured several human dramas, such as a young couple telling their parents that they're pregnant; a man proposing to his beloved in a hot-air balloon; and a hiker cresting a mountain. Each moment of emotional, breathtaking triumph was accompanied, nay, made possible, by the presence of Coca-Cola. Grown men cried through that movie. (I cried too, but that's not newsworthy.)

We get the message that Coca-Cola is essential in life's most precious moments. It's essential to the happiness of pregnancy, a successful marriage proposal, a physically exhausting achievement. And we buy it, literally and figuratively!

One decluttering guru tries to motivate us to purge our excess stuff, asking us to look around our homes and remind ourselves: "All this junk used to be money." We buy stuff we don't need in the pursuit of happiness, then try to become happier by purging it all, then buying new stuff to fill the void. Again, good for the economy; bad for happiness.

Another obstacle to happiness is the presence of too many options. Psychologist Barry Schwartz, in his book *The*

Paradox of Choice and in his TED talk, argues that the abundance of choice in the modern era makes us deeply unhappy, even while it presumably offers flavors of happiness.[14] The TED website summarizes:

Why is it that societies of great abundance—where individuals are offered more freedom and choice (personal, professional, material) than ever before—are now witnessing a near-epidemic of depression? Conventional wisdom tells us that greater choice is for the greater good, but Schwartz argues the opposite: He makes a compelling case that the abundance of choice in today's western world is actually making us miserable.

Schwartz believes that infinite choice is paralyzing and exhausting for the human psyche. It leads us to set unreasonably high expectations, question our choices before we even make them and blame our failures entirely on ourselves. His relatable examples, from consumer products (jeans, TVs, salad dressings) to lifestyle choices (where to live, what job to take, who and when to marry), underscore his central point that too much choice undermines happiness.

Two thousand years ago, the rabbi Ben Zoma called it as he saw it: "Who is wealthy? One who is happy with what he has."[15] Yes, happy. With what he already has. With the jeans, TV, and salad dressing already in his closet, living room, and fridge.

I remember trying to choose a white paint color to paint the wooden trim of our home when we moved in. The dizzying options of white made my head spin. Even now, years later, when I look at it, I sometimes wonder: is it the right shade of white? Too many options make us doubtful and envious. Yet we'd probably be loath to give up the variety of choices at our fingertips. Perhaps we can channel our inner Ben Zoma and find joy in our own backyards.

While advertising messages and consumer choices bombard us from without, there is also plenty to sabotage our happiness from within. Let's examine our own attitudes that conspire against joy.

In Chapter 1, I mentioned that often, we are kinder and more patient with strangers than with those closest to us. And similarly, the people and even the things in our lives that ought to bring us the most joy, such as family and health, are not fully appreciated. We are so used to having these things, so oversaturated with them, that we forget to savor and value them.

Dr. David J. Lieberman, in his book, *If God Were Your Therapist*, considers why people seem to be the most grateful when they've stood to lose the most. By way of example, imagine a person in a severe car accident who loses use of his legs for months. With tireless work and painstaking therapy, he regains his ability to walk. He will likely have immense and lasting gratitude for this subsequent ability to walk, as Dr. Lieberman puts it. But now imagine the same person swerved and narrowly avoided the car accident. He'll feel grateful too, but it will dissipate quickly. What's happening here is a phenomenon Dr. Lieberman describes as "perspective" and "entitlement." Because we assume we'll be fine, we feel entitled to that, and that becomes our perspective. Being okay is so commonplace, we forget to let it bring us joy.[16]

Should we be any less grateful for miracles that happen regularly?

Sunrises, sunsets, mountains, valleys, breathing, using the restroom easily (don't laugh)—these are all miracles that happen so routinely that we fail to recognize them as miracles at all. That's why Judaism recommends saying at least 100 blessings a day! There's a blessing for being able to straighten your body in the morning. A blessing for your morning coffee. A blessing for seeing the ocean. And yes, a blessing after using the bathroom.

The blessings remind us that God is the generous provider of all these miracles that happen every moment all around us. The blessings remind us that these events are neither lackluster nor insignificant, but rather targeted expressions of love from God to us. They are gifts created just for us. This perspective is designed to bring us joy.

The final obstacle I'd like to examine is making comparisons. We already discussed the damage that envy can do, and one way to combat that is to stop obsessing over what other people have. To stop obsessing, we have to stop comparing.

Mrs. Tova Leibowitz, a teacher of mine from seminary used to say, "The recipe for unhappiness is compare, compare, compare!" This was before the era of social media where we have the luxury (or the misery) of comparing ourselves to millions of people we've never met and never will meet. I think most of us social media users, if we're honest with ourselves, will admit that frequent use of these platforms brings unhappiness and envy in its wake.

The story of Sam Polk is a sobering one. In a *New York Times* article, Sam describes his life as a former bond and credit default swap trader (please do not ask me what this means). He says:

At 25, I could go to any restaurant in Manhattan—Per Se, Le Bernardin—just by picking up the phone and calling one of my brokers, who ingratiate themselves to traders by entertaining with unlimited expense accounts. I could be second row at the Knicks-Lakers game just by hinting to a broker I might be interested in going. The satisfaction wasn't just about the money. It was about the power. Because of how smart and successful I was, it was someone else's job to make me happy.

Still, I was nagged by envy. On a trading desk everyone sits together, from interns to managing directors. When the guy next to you makes $10 million, $1 million or $2 million doesn't look so sweet.[17]

Sam considers himself fortunate to have recognized the self-sabotaging cycle he was caught in. He eventually chose to walk away from the addictive cycle of envy, greed, and consumerism and the problems they triggered.

In the three years since I left, I've married, spoken in jails and juvenile detention centers ... taught a writing class to girls in the foster system, and started a nonprofit called Groceryships to help poor families struggling with obesity and food addiction. I am much happier. I feel as if I'm making a real contribution.

Notice the connection here between giving and happiness. We talked about generosity back in Chapter 4, and its many benefits. Here's another: Sam was so much happier when he was giving than when he was getting. Envy is focused on acquisition, whereas happiness comes from, among other things, generosity.

There is a reason that, "Thou shalt not covet" is included in the Ten Commandments.[18] There is no end to the bottomless envy that can exist in our hearts. The only way to overcome the obstacle is to follow God's spiritual roadmap and choose happiness.

Susan, Ellen, Brenda, and Andria are a group of friends (two of whom are also sisters) in their 70s who study mussar with me each week. I love hearing their reflections on life and their accrued wisdom. Here are their thoughts on happiness:

Susan says: When asked to comment on how my study of mussar had affected the trait of happiness in my life, I was a bit flummoxed. Certainly, my studies with Ruchi and a few treasured friends have made a perceptible difference in my life and in my relationships, but "happiness?" All I could think about was my work on the trait of gratitude. My (newly acquired) practice of the daily recitation of the "Modeh Ani" prayer, the verbal assertions of the many things for which I am grateful, and my stated intentions of how I will express that gratitude in my actions on any given day, have all added to my happiness considerably. Nothing outwardly has changed. The great difference is in my commitment to recognize my many blessings consciously on a daily basis. In doing so, my happiness quotient has been exponentially increased and that is one more blessing for which I am extremely grateful!

Ellen says: I recall the day my sister called to ask if I wished to join her and two other close friends and begin to study mussar with Ruchi Koval. I had spent much time loving the stories and experiences my niece was enjoying during her study… and I was thrilled!

The joy of learning, reflecting, and absorbing the wisdom of our forebears is awesome!

And more so…. to realize how absolutely contemporary and practical so much is today!

Happy is a choice, I learned indelibly 51 years ago. As a freshman in a dorm, weeks into the semester, I attended a floor meeting. I was the focus of several girls who found me moody! Me???? I was not loving my roommates, finding the adjustment difficult, but had no idea my unhappiness affected anyone but me. I don't recall what or how (never thought of therapy then) but knew I had a choice, and albeit painful at the time. I chose to decide that the girls meant well! I remember it like yesterday, but until Ruchi asked for reflection on "happiness," it was deeply buried. The ability to truly feel happiness, the joys in everyday life, and to realize you make it happen are incomparable!

Sharing each Monday, making the ethics and teachings reflect our present life and goals, with dear and valued friends—that is happiness! Waiting for my husband to ask, "What did you learn with the 'mussar girls' today?"—that is joy!

Andria says: I start my day reciting the Modeh Ani in Hebrew. I never miss a day to say thank you, and I appreciate each day. Gratitude and happiness are interchangeable. What Ruchi has taught about happiness identifies the tenets and the gifts with which I have unknowingly lived, but until I studied mussar, I don't think I fully realized or was able to identify the tenets.

This topic has been difficult as I approach the second anniversary of my beloved and long-lived mother's death. She has been on my mind. Family, love, kindness, thoughtfulness, helping others in the very simple and broad sense, is happiness.

When my father died of a heart attack at 44, it was beyond painful. But I still have great gratitude and happiness that he had a fast death. As a huge cigarette smoker, his suffering could have been so much worse. I am grateful my mom was a strong, daily example of someone who lived, valued and demonstrated a Judaic value system.

I didn't even realize, until studying mussar, that she was modeling our Judaic value system. It's just who she was. I understand more fully how our family was enriched by times of fun, gifted by wonderful, supportive, loving relatives. Our daily lives were always defined by doing for others; our table always had room for anyone. So here I am back to my simple takeaway: happiness = gratitude.

AFTERWORD

And so, my mussar mates, we have come to the end of the book and to the beginning of the journey. You will notice many "mussar moments" as you go through your day—previously known as "triggers" or "annoyances" and now apparent as opportunities to strengthen your mussar muscles and grow into a more fully evolved, better person.

We learned about judging others favorably, and how being judgmental harms us. We explored three levels of judging favorably, from creating a backstory, to seeing the bad thing as something good, and finally, to learning to look at others with unconditional love.

We discussed forgiveness and delved into the Torah origins of this deeply human act of redemption. We distinguished between "good" and "bad" apologies and taught how to apologize effectively. We laid out the six steps of forgiveness, and finally, we arrived at the possibility and promise of forgiving oneself.

In Chapter 3, we faced the difficult but very rewarding task of accepting others, just as God unconditionally accepts us. We delved into the difference between conditional and unconditional love, and we looked at how acceptance makes relationships thrive.

We then focused on generosity, exploring how we can become givers in our interactions with other human beings. Generosity, we learned, is a vital ingredient in creating emotional intimacy. Learning to become generous helps us understand that actions speak louder than words, and also helps us choose love. Being other-focused also helps us achieve long-lasting, satisfying relationships. In this chapter we also discussed how these choices and this ability to give helps us bond with other people.

In Chapter 5 we took a deep dive into the power of speech. We learned how deeply words matter, how powerfully words can help and heal through validation and critiquing others sensitively, carefully and mindfully, and only doing so when necessary. We also looked at how we feel when we are being criticized, and how we can use both wanted and unwanted criticism as a means to grow.

Silence is the flip side of speech, and in Chapter 6, we explored the benefits of waiting to react, creating space between an irritating or triggering action or statement and our response. Summoning the self-restraint to remain silent, and asking ourselves if what we're about to say or do is going to help or hurt, further strengthens us. We also discussed the "extroversion trap," the problem of gossip, and how extremely careful we must be before giving rebuke to others.

As we closed in on our final traits, in Chapter 7 we took a look at the gift of renewal—how to reinvent oneself when we've messed up. We discussed how when the process is engaged in wisely, it is powerful and healing, bringing us to a better place than where when we started. We distinguished between guilt, regret, and shame, and explored how each one affects our ability to renew ourselves.

And finally, we learned that, like love, happiness is a choice. We achieve it via gratitude, which is woven into the fabric of our daily lives through Jewish teachings. We achieve it via faith and acceptance that everything happens for a reason. And we saw how laughter can get us through life's tough times and allows us to retain joy.

Developing these traits can be life-changing, but it takes hard work. We each have aspects of our personalities that can block our way to strengthening these "spiritual muscles." We may have a hint of arrogance, or a lack of self-awareness. We may be impatient, perhaps a little lazy. If you're like me you may have the tendency to prioritize efficiency over intimacy. Perhaps we are insecure, and lack the courage to change. We may easily feel discouraged or struggle with self-control. And the cultural messages all around us, which emphasize materialism, chasing after fame and honor, and self-indulgence, also work against us.

But as I think you've gathered from all the testimonials here, *the journey is more than worth it*. You can do hard things—that's how you will become the best version of yourself. That's why you were put onto this earth, to accomplish. To polish your inner diamond, and to change the world.

Which brings us right back to where we started, but now you truly understand:

"When I was a young man, I wanted to change the world. But I found it was difficult to change the world, so I tried to change my country. When I found I couldn't change my country, I began to focus on my town. However, I discovered that I couldn't change the town, and so as I grew older, I tried to change my family. Now, as an old man, I realize the only thing I can change is myself, but I've come to recognize that

if long ago I had started with myself, then I could have made an impact on my family. And, my family and I could have made an impact on our town. And that, in turn, could have changed the country and we could all, indeed, have changed the world" (Rabbi Yisrael Salanter, founder of the Mussar Movement).

ACKNOWLEDGEMENTS

Thank you Audrey, who started it all, and to all my mussar students both local and virtual. You have changed my life for the better. Thank you to every single person who asked me, after a lecture or class, "Is this in a book somewhere?" You made this happen.

Thank you to Rabbi Yisrael Salanter, of blessed memory, for formalizing the study of mussar, and to modern-day teachers and authors of mussar who have disseminated its study for contemporary audiences, particularly Dr. Alan Morinis.

Thank you Rabbi Daniel and Susan Lapin for believing this book could and should be written, and for coaching me through its many revisions.

Thank you to my dear husband, Sruly, and to our kids, for your patience during the writing process and for always telling me it didn't need to be improved any further because it was, at each stage, perfect as is. Thank you to our parents for always believing in me and supporting my writing.

Finally, thank you to the One Above for giving me the ability, the drive, the words, and the passion, to be a vessel for your light. I only pray I am a worthy refractor.

I would like to thank my tireless editor, Judy Gruen. Judy, you advised me way back when this book was but a twinkle in my eye, and I was honored to have your professional hand and wisdom in its final stages. Thank you for your warmth, excitement, and expertise.

Thank you Rabbi Daniel and Susan Lapin for believing this book could and should be written and for coaching me through its many revisions. Thank you as well for introducing me to the phrase 'ancient Jewish wisdom' that I use in this book.

FOOTNOTES

Chapter 1: Favorable Judgment

1. Leviticus 19:18.
2. Exodus 20:17.
3. Rick Hanson, *Hardwiring Happiness: The New Brain Science of Contentment, Calm, and Confidence* (NY: Harmony Books, 2013), p. xxvi.
4. Daniel Goleman, *Focus: The Hidden Driver of Excellence* (NY: Harper Paperbacks, 2015), p. 172.
5. Leviticus 19:18.
6. Sifra, Kedoshim, 4:10-11; Babylonian Talmud, tractate Yoma 23a.
7. Psalms 121:5.
8. Rabbeinu Bachya, Genesis 2:4; Babylonian Talmud, tractate Shabbat 151b; Babylonian Talmud, tractate Rosh Hashanah 17a.
9. Leviticus 19:15.
10. Yehudis Samet, *The Other Side of the Story* (NY: Mesorah Publications, 1996).
11. Ethics of the Fathers 2:4.
12. Babylonian Talmud, tractate Berachot 54a.
13. Ethics of the Fathers 3:14.
14. "My God, the soul which you have given me is pure," Jewish daily prayers.
15. Tanya Chapter 6.

Chapter 2: Forgiveness

1. Exodus 32, Midrash Tanchuma, Ki Tissa 31.
2. Vilna Gaon on Shir Hashirim 1:4.
3. Maimonides, Laws of Repentance 2:9.
4. Maimonides, Laws of Repentance 1:1.
5. John E. Sarno, MD, *Healing Back Pain: The Mind-Body Connection* (NY: Warner Books, 1991).
6. Proverbs 14:30.
7. Ethics of the Fathers 4:15.

Chapter 3: Accepting Others

1. The Way of God 3:3.
2. Pirkei D'Rabbi Eliezer 29.
3. The Ways of the Righteous, Feldheim English-Hebrew edition, Gate of Love p. 104-105.
4. William Glasser, MD, *Choice Theory: A New Psychology of Personal Freedom* (New York: HarperCollins Publishers, 1999).
5. Anne Lamott "12 Truths I Learned From Life and Writing," April 2017, TED video, 15:46, https://www.ted.com/talks/anne_lamott_12_truths_i_learned_from_life_and_writing#t-280684
6. Ethics of the Fathers 6:6.
7. Genesis 1:26.
8. Ethics of the Fathers 3:14.
9. Rashi on Genesis 32:9.
10. Babylonian Talmud, tractate Bava Metzia 62a.

Chapter 4: Generosity

1. Rabbi Eliyahu Dessler, *Strive For Truth!* (Spring Valley: Feldheim Publishers, 1978), part 2, pp. 141-142.
2. Genesis 1:28.
3. Book of Education (Sefer Ha-chinnuch), mitzvah 1 based on Genesis 1:28.
4. Mort Fertel, *Marriage Fitness: 4 Steps to Building & Maintaining Phenomenal Love* (Baltimore: Marriage-Max, Inc., 2004).
5. Genesis 2:24.
6. Dennis Prager, "The Role of Luck—Thoughts on a Birthday," The Dennis Prager Show (blog), August 3, 2010, https://dennisprager.com/column/the-role-of-luck-thoughts-on-a-birthday/ .
7. Ethics of the Fathers 5:23.
8. Rabbi Eliyahu Dessler, *Strive For Truth!* (Spring Valley: Feldheim Publishers, 1978), part 2, pp. 141-142.
9. Genesis chapter 29.
10. Jeremiah 31:15-16 and Midrash Pesichta Eichah Rabbah 24.
11. Book of Education (Sefer Ha-chinnuch), mitzvah 16 based on Exodus 12:46.
12. http://mentalhealthandhappiness.com/updated-solving-circle/.
13. Ethics of the Fathers 1:17.
14. Ethics of the Fathers 1:15.
15. Gary Chapman, *The 5 Love Languages: The Secret to Love that Lasts* (Chicago: Northfield Publishing, 2015).
16. Babylonian Talmud, tractate Berachot 58a.
17. Ethics of the Fathers 5:23.

Chapter 5: Positive Speech

1. Babylonian Talmud, tractate Arachin 16b.
2. Psalms 91:15.
3. Shemot Rabbah 2:2.
4. Brene Brown "Brene Brown on Empathy," December 2013, YouTube video, 2:53, https://www.youtube.com/watch?v=1Evwgu369Jw.
5. Leviticus 19:17.
6. Kitzur Shulchan Aruch 29:16-17.
7. Chazon Ish, Yoreh De'ah 2:28.
8. Ed Catmull, "How Pixar Fosters Collective Creativity" *Harvard Business Review,* September, 2008, https://hbr.org/2008/09/how-pixar-fosters-collective-creativity.
9. Ethics of the Fathers 1:6.
10. Ways of the Righteous, Feldheim English-Hebrew edition, Gate of Love p. 114-115.
11. Ethics of the Fathers 6:6.
12. Ethics of the Fathers 4:1
13. Rabbi Noach Orlowek, *My Child, My Disciple: A Practical, Torah-based Guide to Effective Discipline in the Home* (Jerusalem/New York: Feldheim Publishers, 1994), chapter 4.

Chapter 6: Silence

1. Ethics of the Fathers 3:17.
2. Proverbs 17:28.
3. Ethics of the Fathers 1:17.
4. Rabbi Akiva Tatz, *The Thinking Jewish Teenager's Guide to Life* (Southfield: Targum Press, 1999), p. 80-81.

5. "My God, the soul which you have given me is pure," Jewish daily prayers.
6. Exodus 34:6-7.
7. Ethics of the Fathers 4:1.
8. One edition I like is: Rabbi Moshe Chaim Luzzatto, *The Path of the Just* (Jerusalem/New York: Feldheim Publishers, 2004).
9. Translation is paraphrased, but corresponds to p. 14-15 in the above edition.
10. Rashi on Deuteronomy 1:3.
11. Susan Cain, *Quiet: The Power of Introverts in a World That Can't Stop Talking* (New York: Broadway Books, 2013).
12. Cain, *Quiet,* 4
13. Cain, 50
14. Cain, 169
15. Ethics of the Fathers 5:7
16. Iggeres HaGra, paragraph 9.
17. Babylonian Talmud, tractate Bava Metzia 58b, but this precept appears many times, elucidated by Maimonides, Rabbi Jonah ben Abraham of Gerondi, The Book of Education, and others.
18. Babylonian Talmud, tractate Shabbat 31a.
19. Ethics of the Fathers 2:4.
20. Babylonian Talmud, tractate Yevamot 65b.
21. Rabbi Mitterhoff, https://globalyeshiva.com/017-negotiate-using-silence/
22. Ethics of the Fathers 4:1.
23. Iggeres HaGra, paragraph 9.

Chapter 7: Renewal

1. Rabbi Abraham Isaac Hakohen Kook, Orot haTeshuvah 5:6. Translation adapted from http://rechovot.blogspot.com/2010/08/rav-kook-on-teshuvah-healthy-natural.html.
2. Babylonian Talmud, tractate Berachot 34b.
3. Kol Eliyahu, parshat Emor.
4. Proverbs 24:16.
5. Maimonides, Mishneh Torah, Hilchot Teshuvah, chapter 2, law 3. .
6. Julee Wilson, "Tracee Ellis Ross Gets Glam For Uptown Magazine 'Hollywood' Issue," Huffington Post (blog), March 1, 2012, https://www.huffpost.com/entry/tracee-ellis-ross-uptown-cover_n_1314471
7. Brene Brown, *Daring Greatly: How the Courage to Be Vulnerable Transforms the Way We Live, Love, Parent, and Lead* (New York: Avery Publishing, 2015), p. 69.
8. Babylonian Talmud, tractate Shabbat 88b. Translation mostly by safaria.org.
9. Rabbi Moshe Chaim Luzzatto, *The Path of the Just* (Jerusalem/New York: Feldheim Publishers, 2004), p. 15 and 31.
10. Laura Vanderkam, "Are You As Busy As You Think?" *World Street Journal,* February 22, 2012, https://www.wsj.com/articles/SB10001424052970203358704577237603853394654.
11. Dr. Stephen R. Covey, "The Big Rocks of Life." *Appleseeds.org,* http://www.appleseeds.org/big-rocks_covey.htm.
12. Rashi on Genesis 6:9.

Chapter 8: Happiness

1. Deuteronomy 26:11.
2. Deuteronomy 26: 1- 11
3. Rabbi Dessler, Strive for Truth, part one, p. 26.
4. Rabbi Moshe Chaim Luzzatto, The Way of God 1:2:1.
5. Ethics of the Fathers 4:21.
6. Avot d'Rabbi Nosson 34:9.
7. Genesis 29:35.
8. Jewish daily prayers.
9. The Ways of the Righteous, Feldheim English-Hebrew edition, Gate of Joy, p. 177.
10. Babylonian Talmud, tractate Berachot 60b, translation by safaria.org.
11. Rabbi Dr. Akiva Tatz, "Redeeming Laughter," Chabad.org, accessed on October 19, 2020, https://www.chabad.org/kabbalah/article_cdo/aid/380657/jewish/Redeeming-Laughter-Part-1.htm.
12. Genesis 18:12
13. Babylonian Talmud, tractate Makkot 24b.
14. Barry Schwartz, The Paradox of Choice: Why More is Less (New York: Harper Perennial, 2005).
15. Ethics of the Fathers 4:1.
16. Dr. David Lieberman, If God Were Your Therapist: How to Love Yourself and Your Life, and Never Feel Angry, Anxious, or Insecure Again (New York: Viter Press, 2010), p. 21.
17. Sam Polk, "For the Love of Money," The New York Times, Jan 18, 2014, https://www.nytimes.com/2014/01/19/opinion/sunday/for-the-love-of-money.html
18. Exodus 20:14

Additional Resources
Lifecodex Publishing, LLC

If you are interested in learning more about ancient Jewish wisdom check out our full catalog of resources

Made in United States
Orlando, FL
06 January 2023

28310788R10102